Frank St. Martin

The Silent Healer

A Memoir

Transformation Media Books

Published by Transformation Media Books, USA
www.TransformationMediaBooks.com

An imprint of Pen & Publish, Inc.
Bloomington, Indiana
(812) 837-9226
info@PenandPublish.com

www.PenandPublish.com

Copyright © 2013 Frank St. Martin

All rights reserved.
No part of this book may be reproduced, stored in a retrieval system, or transmitted
by any means, electronic, mechanical, photocopying, recording, or otherwise,
except for brief passages in connection with a review,
without written permission from the author.

ISBN:978-0-9859367-4-7

LCCN: 2013948594

This book is printed on acid free paper.

Printed in the USA

Endorsements

"My wife and I started reading Frank's book and couldn't put it down. It was mesmerizing, magnetic, enchanting and uplifting. Frank also offers readers a technique that anyone can use, at any time, to help heal themselves."

V.P.
Chairman of a $2 billion
investment management firm

"There is a long lineage of great spiritual healers. Among them are Jesus the Christ, Saint Bernadette, and Phineas Quimby. They are separated by centuries. One such healer is alive today, Frank St. Martin. His story of having the ability to help heal people through God and Jesus is incredible. *The Silent Healer* is well worth reading."

Neil C. Carter, Ph.D.
Theological Psychologist
www.drneilcarter.com

"As a longtime Literacy Professor at Rutgers University's inner-city campus, the more I read Frank's manuscript the more I was pleased that I had been asked to read it. Once I started reading the manuscript, I couldn't put it down."

Lucille T. Chagnon, M.Ed.
Literacy Professor
Rutgers University's Camden, NJ campus
Career Consultant
Developer of Literacy Programs
Author of the following books:
Easy Reader, Learner, Writer
Voice Hidden, Voice Heard:
A Reading & Writing Anthology
You, Yes YOU Can Teach Someone to Read:
A Step by Step How-to Book
www.teachtwo.net

"I very much enjoyed reading this book and you will, too. It brought me tears of joy. How refreshing to discover that there are still some genuine people listening to their heart and offering to help others. It is reassuring to know that there are people like Frank St Martin, "The Silent Healer," who received a Gift from God. I was deeply touched by Frank's story. For over 70 years he has helped heal hundreds of people, with a big smile on his face and a strong feeling of having done God's work. Thank you, Frank, for being who you are, an angel from God!"

Jean-Pierre Deluca
Marshfield, MA

"Frank's story is a wonderful example of faith in action. I first met him in a class he took with us years ago and he is truly a gifted healer and someone who lives in the flow of life. This is a book that we all can benefit from reading."
The person who says it cannot be done should not interrupt the person doing it. (Old Chinese Proverb)

Marilou Seavey
MindBridge® Trainings
www.mindbridgetrainings.com

"Frank St. Martin speaks clearly and convincingly of his special gift, as he recounts the variety of his experiences of healing, from childhood to adulthood, with both animals and humans. His wonder at and appreciation for his gift are part of the appeal."

Claudia Tessier, Author
The Surgical Word Book, 3rd edition
The AAMT Book of Style for Medical Transcription,
1st edition
Management and Security of Mobile Devices in Healthcare
Contributor, *mHealth: From Smartphones to Smart Systems*
www.ctessier.com

Dedication

My grandparents, Matilda and William,
for their love and understanding

My companion and friend, Andrianne,
for her constant support and encouragement
for the past 20 years

Introduction

If you could be someone else, who would you want to be? Some would say I would be "so and so" because of the money or the talent or the possessions that man or woman has.

I asked myself the question, "If I could be someone else, who would I want to be?" The answer surprised me. After thinking about it for about five seconds, I knew the answer. I would pick someone exactly like me. Someone who has done exactly everything I have done in my life and believes in God and Jesus as much as I do. I want all my memories, good and bad, because this is who I am. I have little money, but I wouldn't want money, or fame, if I had to lose the memories of those I have loved and those who have loved me.

I grew up very poor, but we stood proud and willing to help anyone who needed help. Where I lived, people cared about one another. Love, kindness and forgiveness are what prevailed in those days.

When I was 8 years old, I started to gently rub the tips of my index finger and thumb together then I would imagine a picture in my mind of what I wanted, and continued rubbing gently. It didn't matter which hand I used. Whenever I did this I would get what I desired. If I had a discomfort in my body I would continue to rub those fingers together and make believe I could visualize the pain within me. The pain would then fade away until it was gone.

Once your subconscious mind believes you, whether the thought is positive or negative, it will carry out your wish. Always be positive about what you want your subconscious mind to do for you. Repeat it several times each day, and before going to sleep, always gently rubbing the tips of your index finger and thumb. I have always used this technique to help myself. It works! All things are possible when you believe in yourself.

As this book is published, I am 80 years old. I am who I am and I like who I am. I like helping others.

Frank St. Martin
June, 2013

Preface

When I was young, I was never sick. I would wonder how it felt to be sick and ask others how it felt but I really didn't know how I would feel. After a lifetime of thinking this way then it happened to me. In 1996, at the age 63, I woke up feeling hot and sick. I got out of bed and ate very little and then went back to bed.

My lady friend, Andi, after looking at me, said, "I'm taking you to the hospital."

"Definitely not."

I continued to feel hot and uncomfortable and was getting sicker each day, but I wouldn't go to the hospital. It was a learning experience for me. *This must be how people feel when they're sick, hot with pain in the stomach. It does not feel very good,* I thought.

Andi came to the bedroom and said, "You're not eating." "Please, let me take you to the hospital."

Although I was able to overcome the pain, I had forgotten about eating and couldn't remember how many days it had been since I had any food so I decided to go to the hospital by myself. I knew Andi cared about me, but if something was really wrong, and I was told I could die, I didn't want her there worrying about me. I would make arrangements to take care of Andi and tell her when it became necessary.

I've had a good life, no regrets. I helped a lot of people in my lifetime and that is all that I really wanted to do. I want to be humble, wise, happy and enjoy life to its fullest. In my next lifetime I want to help more people. *Only good shall come into me and only good shall leave me,* I thought, as I left for the hospital.

A doctor did some tests and referred me to a urological surgeon. The next day, as I sat in his office, the doctor said, "I have never seen as bad a case as this. You must have known you had a problem. Why did you wait so long to see a doctor?"

"I didn't think I had a bad problem."

Then, he said, "Do you understand that you could die from this? It looks like prostate cancer. I have to operate, the sooner the better."

"Okay."

He picked up the phone and made an appointment for me for the next morning for an MRI and said he needed an operating room on Wednesday for surgery on an emergency case.

"You don't look worried or concerned," he said.

"Would it help me if I were worried or concerned?"

"When you leave this hospital you should go to a lawyer and make out a will. I would estimate that you have a couple of months to live. When I operate on you it will give you another month or so. I'm sorry, but you waited too long."

I left his office and walked to my car. I put the key in the ignition and just sat there thinking of what the doctor said and wondered what he could see that was really so bad. *If I must die, then I will*, I thought, *but I really want to live to be a hundred years old so I can continue to enjoy working with healing people. I enjoy my life every day. If the results were bad, I would try to postpone my death or try my best to heal myself.*

As I thought of my diseased prostate, I wondered what a healthy prostate looked like. I wanted the doctor to tell me this so I got out of my car and headed back to see him. He asked if something was wrong.

"Can you show me what a healthy prostate looks like?"

His face lit up. He said, "Come with me."

I followed him into his office and he pointed down at a picture that was under the glass covering on his desk. I studied this picture of a healthy prostate. I shut my eyes and tried to absorb the picture until I could see it clearly in my mind.

I got up from my chair and said, "Thank you."

"That's all you wanted?"

"Yes, now I know what a healthy prostate looks like."

I drove home to talk to Andi. She was waiting in the kitchen and asked how it went.

"No problem," I said avoiding what the doctor told me. "Tomorrow I go for an MRI. They want to check to make sure everything is all right, that's all."

At 7 p.m. I told Andi, "I'm going to bed now to meditate. Please do not disturb me."

"Anything wrong?"

"No."

She knew that I would meditate for long hours for people that would write to me in need of healing.

At 7 p.m. I was sitting up in the bed and meditating to a very deep level. I enjoy this depth of meditation. It is much different than anything I have read, or heard about. I visualized a healthy prostate in front of me, and then I brought this healthy prostate within me to replace the damaged one.

At this level of meditation I go to a place that I use for healing. As far as I can see there are beautiful green rolling hills and rays of light. Just in front of me is a small hill with a well on top. To the right of the well is a bench with a cross cut on each end into the wood. I sat and prayed that I wanted good health. Under the roof covering of the well was a bucket with a rope attached to a handle. I let the bucket go down into the well and brought up the bucket full of water. I saw a ladle and got some water and went to drink from the ladle, but I could not. As my hand brought the water toward my lips my head moved back away from the water. I held my hand steady and brought my lips to the water to drink, but my hand kept moving away from my lips. It was evident I wasn't allowed to drink this water. I put the water back into the bucket then sat on the bench and looked around. It was a beautiful day.

I sat, prayed and meditated on this bench for a long time. I asked for healing then I got up and went to the well and scooped some water from the bucket onto the ladle. I asked God, "Please let me drink some of this healing water from your well." I moved the ladle to my lips and drank the water. It was cool and soothing. I took more water from the bucket and was allowed to drink again after saying, "I thank you." When I returned to my bed, where I was meditating, it was 7:30 a.m. the next morning. I had done 12 and ½ hours of meditation and visualization and I felt good and healthy.

I took a shower and drove to the hospital for my MRI. After I came home, I enjoyed a little work in the yard. At 11 a.m. I went to see the doctor. I sat in his office as he was reading my report on the MRI. He picked up the phone and called down to the office where the test was performed and told them they read the MRI incorrectly. After a few minutes the doctor was told they hadn't made a mistake. He got angry and hung up the phone saying, "They don't know how to read their own MRI." After hearing this I said to myself, "Thank you, God."

Then the doctor said, "We will still proceed with the operation."

I interrupted him and said, "Wait a minute, I want another test done before I will consent to an operation."

"Why would you not want the operation scheduled? The tests that I have done show you have a serious problem. The sooner you have the operation the better it will be for you."

"I understand," I said, "but I want another test."

The doctor did not appear too happy. It meant he would have to cancel the operation.

He made a phone call to someone then turned to me and said, "Wednesday at 2 p.m., be here to have another test. A camera will show us your prostate and a long needle will take sample tissues."

I believe it was six needles and six times they poked and took their samples. The samples were sent out and returned a week later.

One week later I was sitting in the doctor's office waiting to hear the results of the test. The doctor was sitting next to me reading the report from my prostate tests.

"I know you had a serious problem with your prostate. The MRI and this test indicate that now you do not have a problem."

I asked, "Did you make a mistake?"

"No," he said loudly, I did not misdiagnose you. You had a big problem!"

I then took two cards out of my wallet and placed them on his desk in front of him. One card said Certified Hypnotherapist and Reiki Master. The other card said, "Healing with The Mind, The Hands, and The Power of Prayer." When the doctor looked at my two cards he got up quickly, sending his chair rolling toward the wall. He left the room without saying a word.

I waited a long time for him to return. He was very angry when he entered and walked over to his desk. He picked up the two cards, forcibly trying to push them into my shirt pocket. I took the two cards before he tore my shirt and asked him "What is the problem?"

"I don't believe in any of these things."

"Do you believe in God?"

"I only believe in me."

"You are a small-minded person with money first and people second. Do you want to see me again for a check-up?"

"Why? If anything is wrong, heal yourself again!"

I requested that all my records be sent to a doctor in Boston. I left his office, never to return. The doctor in Boston again examined everything regarding my prostate.

This new doctor said, "You're amazing! No problems!"

It is 17 years later and I have never had the problem reoccur.

One

I was born on April 1, 1933 in Taunton, MA. My mother's maiden name was Rose St. Martin. I was named after my father, Frank Bento, Jr. One year after my birth my mother died. My father, knowing he could not care for a baby, asked my mother's parents if they would care for me for a few years. He explained he wanted to go to California, where his mother and brothers lived, to establish himself with a good job and then buy a house. He told them he would come back in three or four years to get me. My grandparents agreed and considered it an honor to raise their deceased daughter's child even if it were only to be for a short time.

My grandparents never heard a word from my father during the years he was gone. Approximately four years went by when one day my grandparents heard a knock on the door and opened it to find my father standing there, and invited him in.

My father saw me and immediately said, "Hi Frank, I'm your father, and I've come to get you. We are going to live in California."

He said he had a good business in carpentry and was making a lot of money and hoped to buy a house soon.

The first question my grandparents asked was, "Are you married?"

"No."

"Who is going to take care of Frank when you are working?"

"Frank will be all right. I have a nice apartment. I will leave him there and lock the door until I come home from work."

My grandmother became upset when she heard my father's intentions. Almost crying, my grandmother looked at my father and said, "No way are you taking Frank, to leave him in a locked apartment all day, alone, until you return from work!"

My father became angry and raising his voice said, "Frank is my child, I will do as I please!"

My grandfather sat across the table and listened patiently until my father had finished talking. He then got up from his chair, looked at my grandmother, then at my father.

"You're not going to lock Frank in any room all day until you return from work," my grandfather said, pointing his finger at my father. "Get a lawyer, we are going to court!"

I remember, while in court, my father was sitting next to a beautiful woman. The judge asked my father if they were married.

"We are getting married."

Then the judge asked my grandparents what had transpired during the four years I lived with them. Once they finished their side of the story, they added, "We raised eleven children and we would like Frank to stay with us."

My aunts and uncles were also present in the courtroom and, one by one, they attested to the judge that their mother and father were good to them while growing up. I remember walking over to my father and his girlfriend, but my Aunt Lillian quickly held my hand, and sat down with me next to my grandparents. I recall my grandfather and grandmother standing in front of the judge, when the judge pointed his finger at each of my grandparents.

"You are the father and mother of this child." I then heard the judge say, "His name will be Frank William St. Martin. Let the records show this, so be it!"

Two

On April 1st, 1939, I was sleeping in my bed when, suddenly, I awoke and heard my grandmother talking to my Aunt Lillian.

"It's 8 o'clock and Frank will be waking up soon. I'll bet he will be very excited. The first thing he will want to know is what presents he got for his birthday."

As I lay in bed listening to my grandmother, whom I now called Meme (and my grandfather was Pepe), I heard her say, "The years have gone by so quickly. Frank is now six years old."

She went on to say she'd raised eleven children but had to say that I was special. My Aunt Lil agreed and said, "We all know there is something special about Frank, but we don't know what it is. You always feel better after talking to Frank. It doesn't matter what you talk about, even if it's only about his toys, you feel better about everything else," including problems which were never discussed.

Aunt Lil then said, "Ma, it's strange, but it's been said by others, too, that you feel good when you are around Frank."

The Silent Healer

As I lay in bed, listening to my Meme and Aunt Lil, I felt good hearing what they had to say. People liked me and I liked people. I listened to hear more, but all I heard was the water running, and the pots and pans being taken from the cabinet. I lay quietly in bed on my sixth birthday, filled with excitement. My eyes soon drifted to a picture on the wall. Every night my grandparents would read the words from this picture to me. I came to know it as The Shepherd's Prayer.

The Lord is my shepherd, I shall not want;
He maketh me to lie down in green pastures.
He leadeth me beside the still waters;
He restoreth my soul.
He leadeth me in the paths of righteousness for his name's sake.
Yea, though I walk through the valley of the shadow of death,
I will fear no evil;
for thou art with me;
thy rod and thy staff, they comfort me.
Thou preparest a table before me in the presence of mine enemies;
thou anointest my head with oil, my cup runneth over.
Surely goodness and mercy shall follow me all the days of my life;
and I will dwell in the house of the Lord forever.
(Psalm 23 - King James Version)

Frank St. Martin

First, I heard these words, then I memorized them, and soon after I could read the words on the picture. I never was afraid of the dark or the noises in the night, I felt as though I was protected at all times. Even to this day, as I write this book, the words and feelings are still with me. I still feel protected.

With thoughts of toys, clothes, ice cream, cake and blowing out the candles, I got out of bed feeling happy with a big smile on my face. Today was going to be a good day. I put on my short pants and a striped t-shirt. As I bent over to put on my socks and shoes, I noticed the light in my bedroom had changed. The light coming into my room from the one window, next to my bed, was sufficient so I hadn't turned on any lights. As I looked up toward the ceiling I noticed that the light now coming into my room was different. Everything looked all right, but I felt I was not alone, although I was physically alone in the room. I knew someone was in the room with me. I looked around the room, but I saw no one. I sat for a while, enjoying the brightness from the light in my room. I remember feeling like my bedroom and I were not attached to this physical house, but were somewhere else being observed. I thought I should go and tell my Meme and Aunt Lil about what had happened in my bedroom.

As I stood up to leave my room, I felt something warm flowing onto my head. It soon covered me from head to toe. As I looked at my arms and my shirt, I could see that I was soaking wet with something red. I slowly walked from my bedroom toward the kitchen, stopping to wipe my face, when I noticed my hair was also dripping wet with this red liquid. It was going into my eyes as well. It looked like blood, yet I hadn't cut myself.

As I walked into the kitchen, I saw my grandmother and my Aunt Lil. They were both busy preparing vegetables for dinner. When they looked at me they both cried out, "Oh my God, what happened to you, Frank?" My grandmother and Aunt Lil, with tears in their eyes, quickly came to me and started to wipe blood from my head and face.

My Aunt Lil quickly gathered a pan of water and towels. They washed the blood that covered me, from my head down to my feet. Meme then took my clothes off and continued washing and wiping me dry. They both kept looking to see where I might be bleeding from, but the blood was not coming from me.

My grandmother asked me, "Where did all this blood come from?"

I told my Aunt Lil and Meme about the white light that had come into the room and, as I was leaving my room, I felt the blood coming down from my head and then it covered me. I added, "It was nice and warm."

My grandmother and aunt looked toward my bedroom and saw a trail of blood and became very afraid. My grandmother held me closer, and Aunt Lil held her mother's arm.

"I'll show you," I said, as we walked into my bedroom.

We looked up and saw there was no blood on the ceiling, but there was a lot of blood on the floor, on the walls and the side of my bed.

"Where did that blood come from?" asked my Aunt Lil. "There is no blood on the ceiling, yet the blood splattered on Frank's head, the wallpaper and everywhere in the room."

My grandmother then looked at Aunt Lil and said, "Don't talk about it. It's not for us to understand. Clean the blood off Frank's feet and I'll get him clean clothes."

As they cleaned me up, Meme said, "Do not tell anyone about the blood."

I sat in the corner of the kitchen, where there was no blood, while my grandmother and Aunt Lil knelt down and prayed; thanking God that I was not harmed. They also prayed to Jesus, and to my mother, to take care of me. Then they went into my bedroom and washed the floor and the wallpaper, removing any trace of blood. They removed the sheets and blankets from my bed, and even when the sheets and blankets were thoroughly washed, my grandmother would say to wash them again and again.

All of my aunts and uncles came to the house to visit that day. They were told of the blood and all that had occurred. After everyone had left, I told my grandmother that I felt that they would now go to church and, as I did, pray for forgiveness and protection.

"You are probably right."

My grandmother and Aunt Lil then went into their bedrooms to change their clothes for church and said we were going to talk to the priest.

We began the long walk to the church in silence as my Meme held my hand. I felt that everything my aunt and grandmother saw they were now reliving in their minds. I thought of the picture on the wall in my bedroom, with the words of The Shepherd's Prayer, and it kept me from being afraid.

Meme went to the rectory to talk to the priest. After a long while, they came out and we went into the church. The priest spoke my name and told me to come to him.

My grandmother, who was standing near the priest said, "Don't be afraid, Frank."

I then walked over and stood close to him. The priest turned to my grandmother and my Aunt Lil and said, "I want you both to be quiet, do not say a word of this to anyone."

My grandmother and my Aunt Lil responded, "Yes, Father."

The priest then looked down at me and asked if I was afraid. I said, "No," but my heart was beating fast. The priest smiled and put his hand on my shoulder.

"Frank, from the moment you woke up in the bed in the morning, I would like you to tell me everything that happened."

I told the priest the entire day's happenings, from hearing my grandmother and Aunt Lil speaking, to everything else that happened that morning, in correct detail, even down to us walking to the church in total silence. The priest just stood in front of me looking down directly into my eyes as I spoke. As I looked up at the priest I recall he looked like a statue, just standing there. His eyes were fixed on me but he did not move nor speak. I looked at my grandmother and my Aunt Lil who looked like statues with their eyes fixed on the priest. No one moved. I couldn't even tell if they were breathing.

I had the impulse to yell loudly, *What is the matter with you?* but I didn't. I remember thinking that I knew how to get home from here, alone! Then I thought, *should I tell my grandfather, who was at work that day, about what happened? If I do, what will he do, become like a statue like them?* I felt like crying as I looked around at the statues, the pictures, and the cross in the church, while I asked myself, *What should I do?*

Suddenly they all moved and the priest said, "Stay right here, Frank," as he went to get a small bucket to fill with holy water.

He began blessing the altar, the door where we entered, up to where we were standing. The priest kept throwing holy water on me. My hair, my face and my clothes were wet. No one said a word, as we listened to the priest praying. I couldn't understand his words because they weren't in English but the sounds of the words were comforting and pleasing.

When the priest finished he said, "Frank, it's a wonderful thing that this has happened to you, but do not tell anyone for they will not understand and could hurt the people who love you. Do you understand?"

"Yes sir."

The priest smiled, patted me on the head, looked at my grandmother and aunt and said, "Repeat nothing about what has happened. Frank is special and others will not understand. You can tell Frank when he is old enough to understand."

My grandmother and aunt then thanked the priest, and we left through the same door we entered. As we walked toward our house, my grandmother and aunt had a lot to say. It was really the same thing over and over.

"Frank, do not tell anyone you saw a priest. People will not understand what has happened to you, and it cannot be told to anyone. You must be silent."

This was the first time I had ever heard these words but it certainly wouldn't be the last time I would hear "Be silent."

Three

I woke up in the morning knowing it was April 1, 1941, my eighth birthday. After I read The Shepherd's Prayer, I just lay in bed, listening to my grandmother, uncles and aunts talking about going to the beach. I was anxious to go and ready to run out of my room and ask Meme to find my bathing suit. All of a sudden I sat down on the edge of the bed. I couldn't move; the excitement within me just stopped. I felt calm, very calm. I wanted to move my arms and legs but I couldn't. I could only move my head and eyes. My attention was drawn to the ceiling and I had the feeling the blood would come down on my head again. I remember saying, *Not again!*

I thought of Meme and Aunt Lil and how afraid they were and how hard they had worked at cleaning every trace of blood from my room. I don't know where I had ever heard these words, or maybe I made them up myself, but my next thoughts were these words, *God be with me and I with you.*

I could move again so I ran out of my bedroom and into the kitchen and announced that I wanted to go swimming. Everyone laughed, and wished me a "Happy Birthday."

I had a good day at the beach. Later in the evening we had cake and ice cream and I received lots of presents. Before bedtime, when everyone had gone home, I told my grandmother what had happened that morning.

"I had the feeling that there was going to be more blood coming down on my head again. I couldn't move but when I said, 'God be with me and I with you' then everything seemed to be all right."

My grandmother hugged me and said, "Be silent, tell no one."

That night, as I lay in my bed, I said a prayer and asked that the blood wouldn't come down on my head again. I slept very well that night, and woke up with a smile on my face. When I woke I questioned myself, *Why am I smiling?*

I tried to remember my dreams, but I could not remember even one. I got out of bed, washed and ate my breakfast then went outside. I sat on the back step, closed my eyes and put two fingers together on each hand. I then relaxed deeply. It was about ten minutes before I opened my eyes. I felt different somehow. I felt relaxed and pleased. I have had this feeling every day in my life since then.

Four

When I was a child, I had imaginary friends, as many other children do, who made me laugh, made me happy, played with me and protected me.

My grandmother would always ask, "Is everything all right?"

"Yes, everything is fine."

I would tell only my grandmother about some of the young children I was playing with that day as their fathers and mothers were watching us.

"What do your friends look like? What are their names? What did their fathers and mothers do while they were watching all of you?"

"They said play nicely, and enjoy yourselves."

I told my grandmother there were times when I was told to go and sit on the porch because a dog was coming down the street behind our house and he would walk through our yard. The dog was not a friendly dog so I was told to stay quiet on the porch until I was told it was all right to come and play again.

"When this happens, where do all the children go? And where do the mothers and father go?"

"Everyone would be gone. They wouldn't come back until that dog walked through the yard and out the side opening in our fence."

Upon hearing this, my grandmother said, "Be silent, tell no one about your imaginary friends."

Usually I would tell my imaginary friends I would see them tomorrow and they would smile and wave to me, as they always did before. Then came the day when I was playing outside and looking for my friends and I asked,

"Where are you? Come play with me."

I looked all around the yard for them and then sat on the back steps and waited for them. I went into the house and told my grandmother that the friends that I can only see are gone.

My grandmother said, "They had another place to go; some other boy to make happy." I accepted that answer. I never again saw my friends.

"Don't worry, everything will be okay," my grandmother said. "You will have new friends. Everyone will be able to see them and talk to them."

Meme was right. Soon I did have new friends to play with who lived close by.

Another thing I did when I was younger was to show my grandmother the birds that I helped to fly or fixed their legs, and the ants, bees, grasshoppers, rabbits, dogs and cats that I had helped. I would see something wrong and I would help them, or at least I thought I was helping them. I remember I used to blow on them, slowly and for a long time, to warm them with my breath. It seemed to help them. Most of the time I helped cats that would come to let me pet them, but on occasion I would help a rabbit. I would also help the birds if they had a string wrapped around their feet or something coming out of their mouths, or tar or gum stuck to them. I always thought these animals would come to me for help.

When I told my grandmother about helping the animals she said, "Be silent, tell no one that you have been healing."

I always said I wouldn't tell anyone, and that always brought a smile to her face.

****

I didn't see my father for many years while I was growing up.

One day, I started walking home from school when my father opened his car door and said to me, "Frank, I'm your father, get in and I will give you a ride home."

Every once and awhile, he would show up and drive me home from school and would always tell me the same story that I was his son and my name should be Bento, Jr., not St. Martin. I would just sit there and listen. My grandparents would invite my father into the house to eat or just to have a cup of tea. I remember

The Silent Healer

my grandfather telling my father they would never deny him seeing me, as long as he didn't try to take me away from them. I recall being very proud of my grandparents; they always showed love, kindness and understanding to everyone.

The one thing I never told my father was about my healing. As I got older, I could recognize my father's anger every time he talked to me. It wasn't important to him that I called him Dad, but that my name should be Bento, Jr. and not St. Martin.

Five

I heard my grandparents talking in another room. It was about my grandfather being sick and having a badly burnt foot. He was unable to work and the bills were piling up with no money coming in to pay them.

I heard my grandfather say, "What can we do?"

I went outside and started raking the lawn. I believed anything would help the situation and, even though I was only 8-years-old, I was trying to help. I began to think, *no money is going to come into our house because I am raking the lawn.*

I went into the house and said to my grandparents, "I know we don't have any money. I could go to work. I can cut and rake the grass, feed chickens and clean the coops."

My grandfather was 6 ft. 3 in. and was a very strong hard working man, yet as I looked at him I could see him wiping away tears.

"Frank," my grandmother said with a crack in her voice, "Everything will be all right," and then they both hugged me.

"Go out and play," Meme said, "Don't worry about a thing, everything is going to be all right."

I was going to tell my grandmother that I was going to ask for help, but I knew she would have said, "Tell no one."

As I was walking to the backyard, I was asking God for help for my grandfather and grandmother. I sat on the step and soon I was somewhere with beautiful lights around me. I thought I was sleeping. When I opened my eyes I decided I better get back to raking the yard. A short time later, I heard a voice say, "Go down into the cellar."

I dropped the rake and went to the cellar, put the light on and, there in front of me, I saw an arm with a hand and a finger pointing to a spot on the cellar floor, and then it disappeared. With a hammer and a screwdriver, I broke the thin layer of cement on that spot. With a screwdriver and a small trowel I dug a wide hole that was at least twelve inches deep. There I found a box in the loose sand. The box was falling apart, but slowly and patiently, I recovered the box in one piece.

Up the cellar stairs I ran into the house yelling, "LOOK WHAT I FOUND, LOOK WHAT I FOUND!" My grandparents came quickly to see what was the matter. I told them I found something that would provide us with money. Why I said this I had no idea, because I didn't know what was in the box that was falling apart. I put it on the table and my grandparents carefully opened it. Inside was a smaller box, wrapped in black plastic sheets. Inside this box was the biggest surprise we had ever seen.

The interior of the box was green and it held two new handguns. They looked like dueling pistols or pirate guns.

"Where did you get this?" my grandparents asked.

I told them about hearing a voice telling me to go to the cellar where I saw an arm with a hand and a finger pointing to the spot where the box was hidden. My grandparents looked at each other, mumbled a few words in French, then my grandmother asked that I go out to the porch and just sit for a little while.

"Don't talk to anyone," she insisted. "Your grandfather and I will talk to you in a few minutes. Just stay on the porch."

When I was called to come back into the house my grandfather said, "Frank, what you have found is worth a lot of money."

They both agreed that the guns should be put away and given to me when I was older.

"You know we don't have much money to give you when something happens to us. We are going to a lawyer to have these guns put in a trust for you. They will be returned to you when you are 21 years old."

I told my grandparents, "I was led to where the guns were buried, not for me, but for us."

After praying about it, we went to the church and told the priest what happened. He told me to tell no one about what happened and then blessed me with holy water and said I did a good thing.

The guns were sold, I don't know for how much, but enough to pay all the bills, buy another car and put money in the bank.

My uncles spent days digging in the cellar, but found nothing. They complained that their backs were sore, and they had blisters on their hands. They were always asking me where I thought something might be buried.

My answer, while laughing was, "I told you nothing more is here!"

Six

On Saturday, I usually liked to go to the town swimming pool. I could swim but not that well, so I practiced swimming in the small pool until I could qualify to swim in the larger pool. Although I knew it was too much for me then, I knew one day I would be able to swim across the pool easily.

While swimming and playing tag with some friends in the small pool, I heard a voice, "Save him, he is in the corner of the pool." I was in the middle of the pool so I asked, "Which end should I go to?" Somehow I just knew, and went quickly to the left corner of the pool. While holding my nose I went underwater. I kept my eyes open and I saw a young boy lying on the bottom, in the corner of the pool. I lifted him up so his head was above the water and yelled for help.

The lifeguard saw what was happening and quickly came, took the drowning boy, and worked on expelling water from his mouth. The ambulance came and the paramedics took the boy to the hospital. Later that day we found out that the boy was all right. Hearing the news, I felt good inside. No one praised me, not even a thank you, but that didn't bother me. I really didn't need praise or a thank you. I knew what I had done and that was all the thanks I needed.

I thought of going home, but before I did I wanted to try out the big pool one more time. It had a diving board that I wanted to jump up and down on and dive into the water, but until now, it was only wishful thinking.

I approached the lifeguard and asked, "Could I try out one more time?"

"You try out every week and I don't think you are ready yet." Then the lifeguard looked down at me and said, "Yes, go ahead and try."

Somehow, with renewed strength and swimming ability, I swam across the pool and back easily. I couldn't believe how easy it was for me to swim, it just came to me. I swam better than I ever had before.

The lifeguard asked, "What has happened to you? Now you can swim as well as anyone in this pool. You certainly have passed the test."

I was extremely happy as I gathered my clothes and headed for home to tell my grandparents everything that had happened. My grandmother asked if anyone thanked me for what I had done.

"No."

My grandmother told me I was thanked because now I have the ability to swim in the larger pool.

I agreed and said, "Even if I didn't make the big pool, I was happy enough just having saved the boy's life. No one has to know that I did this; but I know, and that's enough for me."

Seven

Early one morning I woke up with a thought and a vision of how to build a ladder. With all the boards and nails that were in the backyard of my house, this wasn't going to be hard to do. After building the ladder I put it up against the back of the house, and then lined it up to where I could grab hold to the edge of the roof and shingles. Slowly I climbed up the ladder, grabbed onto the edge of the roof, and scaled the steep rooftop, proceeding until I could sit with my back against the chimney. My eyes slowly closed and the palms of my hands faced upward touching the tips of my thumb and index finger on each hand. I didn't know why I did this; it just felt like something I should do. This was when I began meditating, although I didn't know it was called meditation at the time. I had never heard the word or of anyone else doing this. I received images and colors and experienced a comfortable feeling, as though someone was watching and protecting me.

After about a half hour and, sometimes up to an hour, I would then move to the top of the roof and sit with my legs hanging over the side of the house. Once there I would meditate the same way I had before. Throughout the summer months I would go to the rooftop, sit and meditate. No one saw me go to the top of the roof or come down, although sometimes I sat for hours and did so every day.

While meditating I could feel someone touching my shoulders, my arms, my fingers, or my face, yet when I would open my eyes, I would never see anyone. All I could see, when I turned quickly, was a black line and then it would disappear. I always thought and still do, that it was a doorway to another place. Sometimes, rather than sit on the roof top, I would go to the bank of the river, near where there was moving water flowing over a dam with pond lilies and flowers growing along the edge. It was a beautiful sight. The ducks would paddle around the small island, looking for food. So many things to look at here, I could easily be relaxed. I would close my eyes and soon I would be somewhere else, or I would be enclosed in a large bubble on my way to somewhere nice.

One day, a neighbor saw me sitting on the peak of the roof, with my legs dangling over the edge. The neighbor called the police and I was ordered to come down. Once on the ground my grandmother asked me what I was doing on the roof. After explaining that I was meditating and how good it felt she said,

"Do not do this anymore, Frank, and be silent. Tell no one!"

Again I said, "I promise."

Eight

Even though I was only eight years old, I was open to healing all the time. Every night I looked forward to my dreams. Some nights in a dream, I would be asked by a consultation of four healers if I would go with them and heal.

I always said, "Yes," and was the fifth person in the healing.

I would be brought instantly to the bedside of a person who was very sick. I was never asked to pray a certain way. Everyone prayed silently while looking at whomever we were trying to help. I have been asked to join in healings, as the need arose, and always felt it an honor. I gave one hundred and ten percent of myself to whomever we tried to heal.

Before dreaming of helping someone to perfect health, I heard these questions asked in my mind,

"Will you help others heal?"

"Can you walk in the light and not be afraid?"

My response was always, "Yes, I will not be afraid."

After a long time of being asked these two questions over and over again a third question was asked, "Even though you will still be poor, no fame, or money in your young life, do you accept?"

"Yes, I do."

The questions were repeated again, "Do you accept?"

"Yes, I do."

I would always respond the same way. Every night I would go to sleep and then I would be awakened with the same questions.

"Will you help others heal?"

"Can you walk in the light and not be afraid?"

"Do you accept?"

For weeks, the same questions were asked over and over again.

My answer was always, " I accept."

I started to ask, "Do you want me to heal? Please stop questioning me. It doesn't matter that I will be poor and have no money! My answer has always been and will be, 'Yes, I accept!'"

One day I suddenly realized I was not being asked these questions anymore but I was still called upon to heal. I am still called to heal even to this day.

When I am healing with the four people, wherever it might be, I notice that we are all wearing the same style clothing, a robe with a hood, something like a monk would wear. I enjoy helping whenever I am asked.

After a time of healing prayer, there are times when, like a blink of an eye, we are all at different locations praying. It's a different person in a different room. I enjoy whatever good we may be doing to help someone. When I awake in the morning I remember the dreams.

Only one voice asks now, "Would you come with us to heal?"

My answer is always, "Yes."

From that moment on, no one talks. We may do one person's healing or a night of three or four healings, perhaps more.

Nine

I was given a brown and white puppy that was a combination of many breeds. I named him Skippy. My grandparents said, "You can have this dog, but you must take care of him."

I certainly agreed. Looking into the puppy's lively eyes, I could sense a feeling of love and compassion, but there was also something else between us.

One day, as I was lying on the floor playing with Skippy, he walked up to me and looked into my eyes. I looked back into his. It felt like the whole world stood still. There was a connection bonding us together. How long we looked into each other's eyes I don't know. Then Skippy walked away and became the small puppy again, running and jumping, as a young puppy should. For the next 15 years the connection between us was always felt.

One day while walking alone to the store, I passed a house on the corner where a big black and white dog lived. The dog was very vicious and everyone would walk in the street as they walked by the house. As I neared the store, the dog came over the fence and jumped on me. I fell down and put my hands on his throat as he tried to bite my face and neck. I held his head back trying to keep him from biting me. I hollered, "Skippy, help me!"

Although Skippy did not accompany me on the walk, in a short time he was there. I lay in the middle of the road with this large dog still trying to bite me as I tried to push him away. With his teeth coming close to my face, I prayed aloud, "God, please help me."

Skippy jumped on top of the dog, bit him behind his neck and ears, then the dog grabbed my Skippy behind the neck and tore open his back, about six inches in length. Skippy laid on me, shivering and not able to move. As I was being dragged and bounced up and down on the blacktop I yelled for God to help me, and help my dog. My hands and arms became very strong. I had my hands on the mad dog's throat and squeezed as tight as I could. The dog knew he was in trouble and tried to back off of me. I put my legs around his body and held on, still squeezing. A large crowd gathered around me but no one could get the dog loose from me. By now I didn't care, I thought my dog Skippy was dead.

A police officer came and directed two people to separate the dog from me that was now foaming around its mouth. The police officer shot the dog right there in the road. My body was covered in blood, but I was cut only slightly and I had road rash from lying on the street, fighting the dog.

People helped me to get up and I told them that I was all right. I lifted my dog up in my arms; his back was torn open. You could see inside of him. Crying, I walked home with Skippy in my arms, his body was limp, his head hung down. I kept saying, "Please God, he only tried to help me. Please make him better."

When I arrived home both my grandparents came out of the house to see what everybody wanted. Walking behind me there were about ten people, most of whom were crying. The police officer went to my grandfather and told him what happened.

"There have been other complaints about this dog but now he is dead. I think that Frank's dog is dead also."

"No, he isn't, he will live!" I said.

My grandmother led me into the house. I put Skippy on the floor. My grandmother washed and treated all my cuts with medicine. She gave me clean clothes to put on. Poor Skippy. As he lay on the floor, I sat next to him. I put my hands on him and he was shaking and his eyes wouldn't open. I washed his cut with hydrogen peroxide and could see under the skin. I put iodine on both halves of his cut on his back and spring type clothespins on the cut to bring the two halves together.

A doghouse was made for Skippy; this was the first time Skippy would sleep outside. He had always slept with me. I was told it would be better for Skippy if he slept outside. I believed my grandparents so I agreed.

I prayed that night before I went to sleep. I thanked God for helping me and giving me the strength so that the vicious dog wasn't successful in biting me. I also asked that he save my dog from dying. I prayed for the strength and knowledge to save him. I then went to sleep, but a short time later I woke fighting for air. I thought I was back on the road trying to keep the dog from biting me. I took my pillow and blanket and went outside. I went into the doghouse and lay there next to Skippy, holding him as I went to sleep. My grandfather and grandmother woke me early the next morning, as it was getting lighter out.

"I'm not leaving Skippy!" They agreed to let me stay with him.

When I woke up again the sun was shining brighter. I looked out of the doghouse opening and saw my grandparents looking at Skippy and me. I pulled Skippy out of the doghouse and carried him to the porch and put him on the rocker couch and sat next to him. I was told that I should keep trying to make Skippy drink water: if he did not eat or drink he would die. Throughout the day, I would wet a rag and squeeze water onto Skippy's tongue. I would wash his face and the cut on his back.

At night, my grandparents would now let Skippy lie in my bedroom on the floor. I slept on the floor with my dog. I talked to God, Jesus and the angels always asking for the same thing; "You must help my dog, he only tried to help me."

I knew Skippy would be all right. I started to feel warm inside and I knew, from the knowledge coming into me from somewhere, that Skippy was going to live.

Boy was I happy! I told everyone Skippy was going to be all right!

Everyone would say, "I hope so."

By the fourth day Skippy had not moved, he only shivered. I continued washing the cut on his back, his face and mouth. As I patted him and hugged him, I whispered in his ear, "Skippy you're going to be all right. I know this, and I think you do, too."

Suddenly he stopped shaking. He opened his eyes. His tongue started to move in and out. I put water on his tongue and he started to drink. I tried to get him to his feet but he couldn't stand up. I knew, once he started to eat, that he would get his strength back and get up. I thanked God for helping Skippy.

I ran into the house and told my grandparents, "Skippy is all right. He stopped shivering and his eyes opened!"

I ran out of the house saying, "I'm going down the street to tell all my friends that Skippy is all right."

I told two of my friends to tell everyone that Skippy was all right. I rushed right home where I found my grandmother patting Skippy.

I heard her say, "Everything is going to be all right."

My grandfather was in the house cooking liver to grind up and give to Skippy. Every night I would listen to my grandparents praying. They would always ask for Skippy to live, that's the kind of people they were.

I was fortunate that after my mother died my grandparents adopted me. We were very poor, but we were happy doing our best. The doors in our home were always open to those who wanted to talk or eat a meal. Everyone was happy that Skippy was going to recover.

All of my friends came over and so did their parents and their friends. I didn't know a lot of people that came, but they said the same thing, "God bless you, Frank, and you too, Skippy."

I fed Skippy by hand and helped him to drink slowly. With my help Skippy gained his strength. A few days later he was walking, drinking and eating by himself!

Ten

    Starting when I was in third grade, I would come home from school, eat and get my shoeshine box that my grandfather had made, along with my polish, a brush, a rag and Skippy. We would go to the busy street corner, not too far from my house, where I would shine shoes. Before long I had a lot of customers. They knew me because Skippy would always be by my side.

    One day, a man dressed in an Army uniform wanted his shoes shined. As I shined his shoes he kept looking at Skippy. I felt something was wrong so I hurried to finish shining his shoes. I was looking down when I heard Skippy growling. I looked up and the man had his hand spread open just above my head. I put my arms around Skippy's neck to hold him back. His mouth was open, his teeth were showing, his hair was up on the back of his neck, and he was growling loudly. He was no longer a puppy, but a large, well-built dog. Anyone who would seek to harm me would be in serious trouble.

    The man apologized and said he just wanted to see what the dog would do.

"What would you do if I didn't pay you?"

"I would tell my grandfather."

"What would you do if I took your shoeshine box and your money?"

He came toward me with hands reaching out at me.

"I'm going to take your shoeshine box and your money."

I looked at Skippy and thought of the man's shoulder. Skippy immediately jumped for his shoulder, with mouth wide-open, ready to bite. The man turned very quickly to avoid my dog. I told Skippy to stand beside me. Skippy growled and showed his teeth, ready to bite. I could feel the anger in him. *Don't do anything yet, Skippy,* I thought, as I kept my eye on the stranger.

The man stepped back, while looking at Skippy and me, bent over and put the money on the sidewalk and said "This is for the shoeshine and the rest is a tip for you." I told him to back away, as Skippy and I went forward to pick up the money.

"I am not doing your other shoe."

What a surprise the man had on his face, as he looked down, to see only one shoe shining.

"Why did your dog try to bite my shoulder?"

"Because I told him to."

"But you didn't say a word."

"I don't have to, all I have to do is picture in my mind what I'd like him to do, and he knows."

The man looked at Skippy and me with a strange look; then he turned, walked across the street and went into a store.

Skippy and I went down the street to another corner. I didn't want to see this man ever again! That evening, when I went home, I was unaware I was being followed by the Army man. The next morning he came to my house and talked to my grandparents. He told them about what had happened the day before.

I got out of bed with Skippy and listened as he told them he was a dog trainer for the U.S. Army.

"This dog, Skippy, I must have him. I feel he has psychic ability. The Army will pay very good money for this dog."

I ran out of my room, holding Skippy by my side.

"Leave this house before I tell Skippy to hurt you!"

The man agreed to leave.

"Before I go, would you have Skippy get angry at me, and then have him go lay down next to that wall I'm pointing to?"

"Of course," I said, "Don't move. I'll show you."

"Don't talk to Skippy as you do this," he said.

I looked at Skippy and looked at this man. I showed anger in my face, and put a picture in my mind that this man was raising his hand to hit me. Skippy started growling right away. I held onto him as he tried to go after this man. I patted him, then, as he looked into my eyes, I looked at the wall. I pictured Skippy lying down near the wall. I let Skippy go. Skippy went to the wall and lay down, still watching me, but also looking at the stranger, growling.

"See, he did just what I wanted him to do without talking to him. Now you'd better leave."

The man looked at my grandparents and said, "I will pay anything, I promise, I must have this dog."

When my grandparents refused he said in a loud voice, "I could have this dog taken away from you by the U.S. Army."

My grandfather stood up immediately, walked over to the man, and said, looking down on him, "You wouldn't want to do that, would you?"

I remember looking at my grandfather, he was angry. I could tell by looking at his face, he resembled an angry giant, looking down on this small Army man.

The man looked up and said, "I'm very sorry I said that."

He apologized and shook all of our hands as Skippy watched with a low growl.

"I'm very sorry. I didn't mean what I said. There's just something about that dog. I now realize you could never give him up."

He stayed awhile and had tea and something to eat with us. He told us stories of dogs he had trained through the years and that these dogs were pretty intelligent but he never encountered a dog like Skippy. As he was ready to leave, he thanked us for being so kind. He also promised that when he told the story of Skippy, he would not tell anyone where we lived because a lot of people would want to know why Skippy was the way he was. He shook our hands, and wished us well.

As he departed, he looked at Skippy and said to me, "This dog was made in heaven and so were you, Frank."

Frank St. Martin

****

Skippy went to school with me every day. All the teachers loved him and so did everybody else. If it were raining outside the teachers would let Skippy in the building. Sometimes, in the afternoon, they would let Skippy in the classroom. Skippy would lie down next to me. He would always be watching me. He would not move until I told him to.

****

When Skippy was 15, I brought him in for a checkup with the vet who said, "I think you should consider helping your dog out of its everyday pain."

"What do you mean?"

"Old age and many more things are medically wrong that cannot be cured. Skippy is suffering."

It took a long time, and a lot of tears, to come to a decision. I did not want my Skippy to suffer. I told my uncle what the doctor had said to me and he agreed. I loved Skippy very much and did not want to see him suffer. I told my uncle that someday I would like him to take Skippy to the vet, but that he must stay with him until his eyes closed, and to be sure to tell him how much I loved him. With tears in his eyes, he agreed.

As the weeks went by, I talked to Skippy and cried many times. I told him what was going to happen. He knew and tried to comfort me by licking my face as I cried. I helped Skippy into my car every day to take a

The Silent Healer

ride with me. I was spending more time with him as he was always there for me.

One day, when I came home from work, Skippy was not there waiting for me. "Oh God," I cried, "I hope he's in heaven! If any dog can go to heaven, my dog Skippy should certainly go there." A short time later my uncle drove into the yard and started to cry as he came toward me. I started to cry. I knew what had happened.

My uncle told me he stayed with Skippy, who looked content and happy, as the doctor put him to sleep. I felt Skippy knew he would no longer be in pain. He had done his best for all of us who loved him. How fortunate I was to have such a wonderful dog! I hope all dogs go to heaven and I hope to be with Skippy again.

Eleven

My grandparents and I were very poor, as others were in the early 1940s. One of the other jobs I had was working as a "water boy." My job was to walk up and down the long trenches where men labored with pick shovels, and bring them water. I earned 25 cents a week working Monday through Friday and a half-day on Saturday. I was happy to make the money. We were poor and certainly needed it. We were poor in dollars and cents but I felt rich in so many other ways. The healing I did to others was worth more than money. I received good health, happiness, satisfaction and all other good things that could come to me. My grandparents displayed love, kindness, and understanding to all they met in their lifetime. It was a good time to be born. It was a good time to be alive. People cared about people. (Oh, how far we have traveled from those days!)

I had a bicycle that my grandfather had put together for me from different bicycles that were being junked for scrap metal. He painted it blue. It got me everywhere I wanted to go. All my friends had better-looking

The Silent Healer

bicycles but it didn't bother me. I could ride as fast as anyone else.

One day, my two friends said, "Let's go to the movies Saturday."

I had a few days to earn the admission price of 10 cents, which included two movies, cartoons and, sometimes, a free bag of popcorn.

I also used to mow lawns and rake the grass and would charge 10 cents. I looked over at the neighborhood yards but they didn't need cutting yet. When Saturday came, my grandmother asked if I had enough money to go to the movies.

"No, I looked all over for work."

My grandmother said the most they could spare was 5 cents. I didn't know where I could get another 5 cents. I sat on the back porch unable to go to the movies with my friends. My grandmother opened the back door and was surprised to see me sitting there. She asked why I was sitting all alone.

"I'm just thinking."

My grandmother sat next to me and said, "I'm sorry we don't have enough money to send you to the movies." I told her "I don't care since we don't have the money."

My grandmother kissed me on the top of my head and said, "Better things are in store for you in the future."

"Yes," I said, as I jumped off the step and laughed.

That brought a laugh and a smile to my grandmother's face. Just seeing her smile and laugh were worth all the movies I could see in my lifetime.

My friends were waiting for me in the field by my house so I walked over and told them I couldn't go. They were disappointed and looked into their pockets and found five pennies. I thought of going back to my grandmother and asking for the 5 cents she offered but then I thought no, we might need those 5 cents.

I thanked my friends and told them I would still walk with them to the movie theater. We walked toward the theater passing a wooden picket fence on my right hand side. I put my fingers between each picket as I walked past each opening. Suddenly my hand was holding a piece of paper. It was a real dollar bill! I showed my friends and told them I was going back home to give it to my grandmother and ask for 10 cents back so I could join them at the movies.

When I told Meme how I got the money, she gave me 25 cents; 10 cents for the movie, and 5 cents for each friend's popcorn. I ran as fast as I could and caught up with my friends just before they entered the theater and gave each one of them 5 cents, which made them really happy.

After the first movie an ad played featuring a beautiful red bicycle with a few white stripes that would be given away each Saturday at the theater. We had never seen a bicycle that beautiful before. For every nickel you spent on candy or ice cream, you would receive a ticket that would be entered into a drawing to win the bicycle. There was excited chatter throughout the theater. Everyone wanted to win one of

The Silent Healer

those bicycles. There was so much excitement about it that the manager walked up and down the aisles with his flashlight, telling everyone to quiet down and watch the movie.

After the two movies, we went outside and saw one of the four bicycles in the window to be given away. We stood there, along with many other children, just looking and talking about the beautiful bicycle.

I looked around at the crowd of people and then looked at the expression in their eyes, which showed their dreams of owning one of these bicycles. All of a sudden a white and yellowish light surrounded me, and I could see myself helping to get one of the bicycles out of the window. In my vision, Joe, the manager, was helping me get the bicycle I had just won.

"Oh, boy," I said to my friends. "You can tell everyone I'm going to win that bicycle in the window."

As we walked toward home, I was really getting excited. I was picturing myself riding that bicycle.

"I have to get home so I can tell my grandmother and grandfather that I'm going to win that bicycle. Maybe they could take a ride here and I could show it to them."

I told my grandparents that since I had a bicycle, I didn't think about winning one, but then the light came around me and I saw myself riding that new red bicycle.

My grandfather said, "Frank, do you know how many tickets will be in that glass barrel? Your chances of winning are next to nothing. Don't get too excited over the new bicycle, I don't want you to be disappointed."

Frank St. Martin

As we were eating dinner I said, "You should go look at that bike, it's red and I'm going to win the last bike." Nothing else was said as we quickly ate our food.

I worked here and there to make enough money to go to the movies on Saturday. I bought ice cream, 2 scoops for a nickel, and got a ticket for the raffle. I told everybody who would listen to me that I was going to win the bicycle in the window. I put about 3 to 4 tickets in the barrel every Saturday. Between the movies, the large barrel would be brought out. Joe, the manager would roll it around with the attached handle, open the door, and have someone come up from the audience to pull out one ticket.

On the first, second and third Saturdays, a bicycle was given away. By the time we were on the fourth Saturday, I had had about six tickets in the drum. I told the manager, from the beginning, that I was going to win the bicycle in the window. He would wish me luck. I had to laugh because I knew he didn't believe me.

The fourth Saturday finally arrived, and I knew I'd win the bicycle. I was so excited!

My grandfather said to me, "Don't be disappointed if you don't win."

My grandmother commented, "A lot of boys want to win the bicycle. Perhaps they don't have a bicycle, and it could be that their parents can't afford to buy them one. Do you think it would be fair for you to wish you'd win that bicycle when you already have one? The boy that has nothing, maybe it would be good if he won. Do you know what I'm talking about?"

The Silent Healer

"Yes, I do understand." I said, "Maybe the light around me has changed its mind."

"Maybe," Meme said.

On the fourth Saturday, I headed for the theater. My grandmother came with me and I showed her the bicycle in the window. We sat in the middle seats about half way down from the stage. Just before the first movie was over I told my grandmother I was going to go and sit in the front row. Shortly after sitting down my cousin came walking in with her friend who said she would like to have a kiss from me.

"Okay, if you have a ticket to give me for the drawing."

She looked in her small pocketbook and then handed me a dirty looking ticket that she said she had found on the road in front of the theatre. I then gave her a nice big kiss and she was pleased. I knelt down in the aisle near the dim light on the side of the seat. I put my name on the ticket, but it was hard to read because it was dirty.

I ran to the lobby because the first movie had just ended. Joe and another man were already moving the barrel with the tickets toward the stage.

"Wait, I have a ticket to put in the drum first."

Joe said, "Too late."

"Joe, I'm here, I have my ticket."

He stopped, opened up the small door and said, "Go ahead, Frank, put your ticket in here."

I thanked him and went back to the front row and sat down.

The time had come; the drum was being turned around and around. Someone came up, picked one ticket and handed it to Joe. He commented on what a dirty ticket it was and how it looked like the cars had been driving over it. Joe then showed it to the man standing next to him. They both agreed that the first name on the ticket was Frank, then S something, then Mar...

My grandmother stood up and shouted, "Frank St. Martin!"

"Yes," both men on the on stage agreed. They called out my name, "Frank St. Martin, are you here?"

My grandmother rushed down to me and said, "He is right here!"

I got up from my seat and went to the stage. Joe's first comment was, "Well, I'll be."

Joe then told the audience, "This boy told me when we first offered these bicycles that he would win the fourth bicycle, and he did!"

A lot of people yelled out, "He told us he was going to win that bike, too!"

Just like in my vision, I helped Joe take the bike from the window display and rode it toward home. As I got closer to my house, I saw my grandfather driving in his car toward me. I stopped and waved at him and he stopped.

"I told you I was going to win this bicycle."

My grandfather started crying, and so did I. He said, "Frank, your mother is looking after you."

That evening, as we sat for dinner, my Meme said, "I told you about the boy with no bicycle, suppose he would have won this bike. How would you have felt about that?"

"I remembered what you told me. I told Jesus, God and my mother that if that boy has no bicycle, then he can have my bicycle. It's blue and works well. The next time he wants a new bike, he will also have good luck."

My Grandfather smiled and said, "I know someone who has a son who doesn't have a bike. Can I give him your blue bicycle?"

"Yes, please do," I said.

Twelve

When I was 10 years old, I would go ice skating on the river next to my house. I was a good skater, better than most. One day I decided I wouldn't take my skates with me. When I got there, many of my friends were already skating and asked me, "Why didn't you bring your skates?"

"Today, I'm going to slide over the channel to the other side; then I will run and slide back the same way."

With many of my friends watching me, I tried to run on the ice as fast as I could, but it wasn't fast enough and I fell through the ice. I held onto the edge of the hole in the ice looking around as I called for help. Many were watching me, and some came running to see me, but no one would dare venture out to where I was to help me. Only my hands, shoulders and head were above the ice-cold water. I tried to get out but I couldn't. My clothes were wet and heavy and my hands were freezing cold.

An onlooker said, "Go down and push yourself up from the bottom. If you come up fast you may be able to get out."

I thought this was the only thing I could try. I went down deeper and deeper, but I couldn't touch the bottom. The current was moving me farther and farther away from the open hole in the ice. Unable to touch the bottom of the channel, I swam upward and came up under some clear solid ice. I could see figures of people on the bank of the river where I used to sit and meditate.

Looking up I saw small air bubbles everywhere but couldn't get any air. I tried and tried to break the ice but couldn't. I felt myself being pushed by the current again, further under the ice. My body was very cold. I started to sink down, deeper and deeper, into the darkness beneath the ice. I forced my right hand to come forward and made the sign of the cross and prayed, *God, help me! Mother, help me!*

Right then, like out of a fire hose, a large amount of warm water pushed my body out of the water, soaring into the air. Everyone watched, then moved back and some started to run.

"Did you see that? Did you see that?" they said.

I held onto the ice and looked toward the shore. A bright white light formed a cloud tunnel toward a man with a very long pole standing alone on the shore. He pushed the very long pole across the thin ice to me. At first, I didn't see the pole as it approached me. I was looking at the tunnel of white light on each side of me and high above me. When the pole touched me, I looked at the man on the shore who showed me how to grab onto it. He never spoke a word. I grabbed the pole and the stranger easily pulled me to shore.

My grandmother came and grabbed my hand and said, "Let's go home."

I wanted to thank the man who pulled me to shore but he was not there, and neither was the long pole.

My grandparents and I were very religious. Many prayers of thanks were said that night. The next day I asked everyone who was at the river if they knew the man who pulled me to shore with the long pole, but no one saw the man. All anyone could remember was that somehow I came to the shore, and that my grandmother grabbed my hand and took me home.

Every winter I remember the warm water pushing me upstream, then up through the hole, and I think of the man with the long pole who no one saw but me.

Thirteen

In the summer, the river close to our house was covered with white water lilies and purple flowers which gave beauty to the water as they grew out toward the deep channel. Close by the riverbank, across the channel, was a little island with different colored flowers growing everywhere. When the soft wind blew across the island you could smell all the beauty of the island flowers. This was a nice quiet place to come and sit. I would watch the fish swim close to the shore. The birds along the river's edge would sing and chirp their songs. The fragrance of the wild flowers was in every breeze. The water going over a small rock dam would create sounds like beautiful music playing in my ears. I spent many hours at this place, relaxing and meditating.

My friends and I would make a raft with boards and tree limbs. We would play games pretending we were pirates. When someone banged their head or got a splinter, a cut or a bruise, I always sent healing to that person, with good results yet no one knew I did this. Not one of my friends went home because of an injury even though we were always getting cuts and scrapes. I would only tell my grandmother what I did and she would tell me, "Don't tell anyone what you're doing. Their mothers and fathers will not understand and will stop you from playing with their sons."

I believed my grandmother so I was careful never to tell anyone what I was doing. Sometimes, I'd ask my friends if they believed that someone in this world could heal another person from pain or other things.

They would answer, "That's crazy, no one can do that, except maybe a witch."

I knew my friends were different than I but I was hoping just one person was like me. I would tell my friends that I'd heard this story about a healer, who could stop bleeding, stop pain and stop a watch from ticking. It wasn't made up or just something I'd heard, since I could do this; it was just my way of hearing their response. Their answers were always the same. Not one of my friends would say anything nice about a healer, yet their cuts would stop bleeding and their pains went away when I sent them healing energy.

I always liked to return to the river to be alone but I was never really alone. The light that I would be encased in while meditating was warm and enjoyable. The images I would see around me were comforting and produced a wonderful feeling. I thought many times of going through the veil of light but if I crossed over somehow I knew I couldn't come back. The only reason I didn't cross over was because I thought my grandparents were growing older and they would need my help taking care of them.

My grandparents told me, when they'd check on me in my room, they would sometimes see the light around me.

My wise grandmother would say, "Be silent on the things you think you know, ask wisely and carefully to obtain the answers you seek. Remember, you have a gift, use it wisely. Be happy in this physical and spiritual world. Everyone you send healing to will benefit, as you get older the ones you seek out will benefit the most."

My grandparents and I never missed going to church on Sunday. I'd listen to the people pray and I came to believe that their words and thoughts would go into the walls, the chairs and the benches. Everything was penetrated with their prayers, their energy of love and healing. Whatever church I go to, I ask for this good energy of love and healing to come to me, within me, so that I can give this energy away to help others.

God, Jesus, love, healing, kindness and understanding, whatever church teaches this, I want to join it. I believe in the religion that brings peace to our earth, peace and love to everything and everyone. When we stand in front of our maker our hair color, eyes, skin or religion will not be important. What will be asked is, "Were you happy in this lifetime?" Did you help others along your pathway on this earth?" I also maintain that "Only good shall come from you, and only good shall come to you." I believe, if you practice this, you shall receive the benefits.

****

One day I remember asking my grandmother, "Can someone look at where the rain begins and where the rain ends at the same time?"

She responded, "Sometimes when you travel down the road you can see where the rain has ended or began. The road would be dry, then like a line drawn across the road, it would be wet with the rain coming down."

I said to my grandmother, "I have a picture in my mind that half of me is in the rain and the other half of me is in the bright sunshine. Do you think I could ever do this?"

She laughed and said, "Is this what you want to do, or is it something you see yourself doing?"

"I see myself doing this."

"This will come true," she said, "if this is important to you, it will happen."

A few weeks later I was at the river relaxing, listening and waiting for something to happen. I was thinking of the warm light I would be in, and the feeling of a hand touching me, and the light warm breeze touching my cheeks, and then crossing my lips like a kiss from someone invisible. I opened my eyes, looked up at the sky, and saw black clouds forming together quickly. I started to feel the coolness of the air. Just before the dark clouds appeared, there was the sun shining brightly in the sky. As I looked at the river and the trees, everything looked as though a gray light was starting to hide everything, but a flash of lightening came quickly and made the sky and clouds bright for a moment. I got up and started walking toward my home.

As I was standing there looking toward the river, the rain suddenly came pouring down very hard just in front of me. I could see the rain on the blacktop of the parking lot coming toward me, not at a fast pace, but slowly advancing. The vision I had of half of me walking in the rain, and the other half of me in the sunshine, was going to be a reality. I thanked God, Jesus, the angels, my mother and everyone else who had made this come true for me. I had really wanted to do this. Looking down at the blacktop, I moved half of my body into the heavy raindrops. My legs were spread apart; my arms were straight out from my shoulders; one half of me was soaking wet, the other half of me was dry. The sun was bright and warm on one half of me.

My grandfather and grandmother started walking towards me and then stopped. They had tears in their eyes when they saw what was happening. I saw them both bless themselves with the sign of the cross, and then they both walked back to the porch and sat down, wiping away tears.

The happiness that I was enjoying stopped as sadness came over me. I walked into the sunshine as the rain followed me to the porch. With tears in my eyes I could see they were crying and asked what was the matter. They both hugged me, we all cried, and then they said these were happy tears because they saw me get my wish.

As we sat there on the porch, happy together, watching and listening to the heavy raindrops bouncing on the pavement, I thought God must have allowed them to see this happen to me. I looked down on the blacktop driveway and smiled. It was an experience I will never forget.

Fourteen

One morning I woke up from a dream that seemed so real. It was about my grandparents bringing me to another town where there were boats. In my dream, as I went out to one of the boats, I said, "I'll see you soon. I must go where I'm needed." As the boat left the dock, heading out to sea, I waved to my grandparents and sent them love and protection. As the boat continued out to sea I realized I was alone on the deck and I wondered where all the passengers were and why I was there. That's when I awoke.

I got out of bed, washed, dressed and combed my hair. At the age of 14, I wasn't old enough to shave yet. I went to the kitchen where Pepe was cooking my favorite breakfast: steak, eggs, fries, toast and tea, my favorite beverage. While Meme was setting the table, I sat down while my food was being prepared and told them about my dream. My grandmother became concerned and questioned me about whether the boat returned to the dock where it originated.

Without thinking I said, "No, it will never return to that dock again."

"Then what happened to you?" she asked, as she started to get upset.

My grandfather put his hand on her shoulder and looked at me and asked, "In your dream did you come back to us alive?"

"Yes."

My grandmother was now wiping tears from her eyes.

Pepe said to her, "Nothing is going to happen to Frank." As he put two hands on her shoulders, he said, "Frank has never lied to us, has he?"

"No," Meme replied.

"Ok," he said, "It's time to eat. Frank is going out. He will need a good breakfast first."

My grandmother looked at my grandfather and nodded her head in agreement.

After breakfast, I told my grandparents, "I'm going bowling and after that I'm going to the movies with three of my friends and I should be home around 3'o'clock."

The day went as planned and we had a good time. As we started to walk toward home, I decided to visit my Aunt Lil and Uncle Henry who lived close by. As I walked into the yard I saw my uncle, who was a good mechanic, working underneath the car.

As I was walking past the car, I bent down and said, "Hi, if you need me for anything, I'll be in the house with Aunt Lil."

Frank St. Martin

When I entered the kitchen Aunt Lil said, "I saw you coming into the yard. Guess what I'm making for the two of us? I'll give you a hint. It's something you and I used to have often together."

I smiled and said, "Hot cocoa."

We sat together, sipping from the smiley cups we always used, as we spoke of the memories we shared over the years.

Aunt Lil said, "You know, Frank, I was with you throughout much of your earlier life. I was always amazed at all the things that you could do. My mother still tells me about the healings. I can't tell anyone about them; they would think I'm crazy. I've heard you say, 'Of course, I cannot heal anyone.' I thought that you were lying to the people and I told my mother that you were misleading a lot of people about your ability to heal. My mother said, 'Frank is not misleading anyone about healing, he is telling the truth.'"

"Aunt Lil," I responded, "As I've said, it is through God and Jesus that I become an instrument to the power of healing which is sent down through me to help others, and I see miracles happen as people are healed of sickness. Did I do this? Of course not, but I am very proud and happy that I have been picked, in this lifetime, to be an instrument in healing. I do understand when danger is close by and I am not afraid. I feel that I am protected which helps me participate in healing. I wish everyone could understand they have the ability to heal themselves."

Aunt Lil looked up at me with a surprised look on her face and asked me if I would go fishing with Uncle Henry and his friend, Joe. They had leased a large fishing boat to go scalloping and were going to leave the next day. She said she would feel so much better if I would go along with them because she had a funny feeling about her husband going fishing this time. I could tell she was getting upset and worried about Uncle Henry.

I went to where Uncle Henry was still lying under the car.

"Aunt Lil said you're going fishing tomorrow for fish and scallops. Is that hard work?" I asked.

He looked at me and said, "How would you like to come along?"

I immediately said, "Yes!"

Uncle Henry explained we would be gone for four weeks and then come home for about a week, and then go back out fishing again. He said he would pay me for each week depending upon how many scallops and fish we catch.

When we went into the house, Uncle Henry told Aunt Lil he was taking me fishing with him. Aunt Lil was pleased and gave me a wink when Uncle Henry wasn't looking.

Aunt Lil said, "I'll give you a ride home and I'll tell your Meme everything you will need to bring with you. I'm sure she is going to be very worried about your going away for four weeks."

"More worried than you think," I responded. "Wait 'til she tells you about the dream I had last night."

When we arrived at the house, Aunt Lil told my grandmother that I was going to go fishing with Uncle Henry and his friend, Joe. My grandparents were shocked to hear this, but when my grandmother turned and looked at my grandfather he nodded his head yes.

After Aunt Lil left, my grandparents started giving me warnings of what to do, and what not to do, to survive on a boat. I was so fortunate to have grandparents who were loving, caring and understanding. Happy tears came to my eyes as I felt their concern for my safety. As we sat at the kitchen table, I told them I was not afraid and nothing would happen to me.

I also reassured them, "About the dream I had, maybe it wasn't this boat that was going to sink."

In the morning, when I came to the table, a large breakfast was already there for me. My grandparents said everything for my trip was packed and they were going to follow Uncle Henry down to New Bedford where the boat was docked.

"Your grandmother wants us to be with you until you get on the boat," my grandfather said.

When we arrived, my Uncle Henry pointed to a large ship and beamed with pride. It was named the BY CRACKY.

When Joe arrived at the dock, Uncle Henry said, "Ok, let's get aboard, we have a lot of work to do today to get the boat ready for scalloping and fishing."

I was standing toward the front of the boat waving as we said our goodbyes. I thought, *I'm doing the same thing now as I did in my dream.*

Soon we were far from land, heading out further to the open sea. Uncle Henry was looking at a map and then he watched his compass. I looked out the windows and all I could see was water, water everywhere. There were no other boats near us that I could see.

Uncle Henry said, "In about another hour we will be where I believe we will get loads of scallop and some fish."

When we got to that spot, we dropped the weighted steel nets. Every half hour the net was to be hauled in. Joe and I would pull a cord that opened the bottom of the net and all of the scallops and fish were released onto the deck. The cord was then tied back again and Uncle Henry would lift and swing the net out from the boat and then release the cable until the net was back in the water.

Joe and I would throw fish of all different sizes into one of the open holes on deck. The scallops were put in ragbags, tied and then put into the other storage compartment. We worked as fast as we could. The half hour went by quickly, and before long, the net was coming in again. We worked all day into the early evening. By dark we arrived at the icehouse where we would dock and unload the fish. Finally, we were done working for the day and went out to eat.

Each day was the same routine; morning until dark we fished and unloaded the catch, and then we went out to dinner. Early the next morning we'd be off to scallop again.

On the fourth day we left the dock, hearing the engine rumble through the small waves as we continued trying different fishing locations. The further out to sea we went the waves grew higher and higher. I was standing on the bow looking at the water that seemed to be getting darker and darker. I felt something was not right.

Once we started fishing, every half hour, the net was bulging with scallops and little fish. Of all the years he had gone scalloping, Joe said he had never seen such a catch as we were getting hour after hour. We worked very hard. There were so many scallops, the hole was full in no time. We were loading the ship from the front, and down the sides, with bags over bags of scallops.

I noticed lots of fishing boats heading toward the docks. I asked Uncle Henry why they were heading back so early. He said he didn't know.

"It's much too early to quit now," Joe said, "turn the music on and let's dance."

Joe and Uncle Henry were very excited and happy. They caught more scallops and fish in one day than they'd seen in a lifetime. Joe and Uncle Henry patted each other on the back as they both agreed they would never forget that day as long as they lived.

"Don't you think we have enough for today?" I asked.

"Another couple of hours and then we will leave," said Uncle Henry. Joe was excited. He pretended he was tap dancing while he was laughing.

"Let's get some scallops," he told Uncle Henry.

Each time the net was pulled up, it was extremely overfilled. I kept seeing boats heading back toward shore. The next time we were waiting for the net to come aboard I told Joe, "Something is wrong. All the fishing boats we have seen in the past hour have headed toward shore. The waves are getting higher and higher."

Joe didn't hear a thing or pretended he hadn't heard me. He seemed to not care.

"Frank, with all the money you make today, your pockets will be filled and you will have to carry the rest in your hands."

It was of no use to talk to Joe; evidently he needed this money so badly that he overlooked his safety in the process.

The first chance I had I went to Uncle Henry who was singing.

"Frank, you're good luck for us. What we all will make today is more than we will make in a year."

"Uncle Henry, stop and think. The boat is overloaded, the deck is getting closer and closer to the water and all the boats have left. Why? You have been a fisherman for many years. Tell me why they would all leave."

He stood there, dumbfounded, and then he spoke, "Hurricane! Go get Joe, tell him to come here. NOW!"

Frank St. Martin

Joe really didn't want to stop to go see Uncle Henry. He kept working, picking up scallops and putting them into bags. I got very close to Joe and hollered in his ear.

"Right now! Uncle Henry wants to see you, right now!"

Joe now hurried to the steering house and I followed behind him. Uncle Henry was now well aware of the problem we'd gotten ourselves into.

"What was the matter with us? We both have fished most of our lives. Did we see what was happening around us? We didn't want to, we just thought of the money. We paid no attention to Frank. He kept telling us and telling us we were overloaded. The color of the water has changed, the waves are higher, and the black clouds are moving quickly. We are in the middle of a hurricane, Joe! I don't think this boat can weather the hurricane."

"Oh no," Joe said, "I only thought of the money."

We headed toward land. The waves were now 20 to 30 feet high. Large sharks rode the waves next to our boat as the fish and their blood were being washed overboard. Uncle Henry and Joe were holding the large steering wheel.

Uncle Henry kept saying, "We have to stay on course."

He kept looking at the compass. Looking at both their faces, I could see they were frightened.

"Frank, I'm so sorry. I told Lil's mother and father that I would take good care of you! I haven't done that," Uncle Henry mumbled.

"Frank, I'm sorry, it's all my fault," Joe said, "I wanted money and didn't listen to you. I may never see home again."

"Don't say anything negative," I hollered back. "We all will reach land and live to tell the story."

Uncle Henry said, "Lil has told me some of the things you have done. I believe we can make it to shore and be rescued."

"If I had bought a proper radio like I was supposed to, we would have known," Joe said. "We would have heard the coast guard reports."

I quickly said, "Don't feel sorry for yourself. Only think, YES! We are all going to make it to land. We will not be hurt."

"Frank, I don't go to church. I know that Joe and you both go. Can we say a prayer? I will say it, too."

"The most powerful prayer I know is The Lord's Prayer," I said. I started speaking slowly, "Our Father who art in heaven…" Uncle Henry and Joe repeated the words even though the boat almost toppled over.

When we completed the prayer I said, "That prayer was for me, the next 'Our Father' will be for Uncle Henry and the next one will be for Joe."

We went through the prayer two more times. When it was completed I said, "Now we all will make it to land. We all will be saved. I'm going down below for a little while. I will be back soon."

There was so much wind, I had a hard time getting to the door, then opening and closing it. Once at my bed,

I prayed to God, Jesus, my mother and every person I personally knew that had passed away. *It's not only me, there are two other lives here, help them also.*

When I returned to the deck, I got to the top of the stairs and opened the door. All I could see was water; a big wave just washed over our boat. There was a cable from the doorway to the steering cabin. I remembered what Uncle Henry had told me, *Put this on your belt in rough weather and attach it to the cable so you won't be swept overboard.* I felt around my belt and found what looked like a key chain with a snap on the end that goes over and around the cable. Once I was attached I started to walk toward the cabin. Quickly a large wave picked me up, high into the air, and I crashed down hard onto the deck. I almost passed out. I thought the cable had broken and I was pushed up and down again. Uncle Henry saw what happened and came out on the deck, grabbed me by my jacket, and dragged me into the steering house.

It was getting dark outside. Uncle Henry and Joe held onto the steering wheel as hard as they could, following the course that Uncle Henry set for the boat. I asked Uncle Henry about the lifeboat. Uncle Henry threw a switch that was on the dashboard. Lights came on showing the deck and what was left of the front of the boat. Uncle Henry and Joe were extremely tired from worrying and trying to save the boat. I had to change their minds and attitudes if we were all going to survive.

Suddenly I saw lights. "Look!" I said, as I pointed.

"It's land!" Uncle Henry and Joe said.

"I told both of you we would make it to land and live, didn't I?" Uncle Henry's and Joe's faces brightened up.

Uncle Henry looked at where the motor was and saw water accumulating. "When it gets to the coil and spark plugs it will stop running and we will tip over."

The waves were still 20 to 30 feet high.

"We will make it," I said.

"Think of what we can do to get rid of the weight." Uncle Henry said. "Help Joe with the steering wheel."

Uncle Henry went to the deck, first attaching his belt to the steel cable. We could see him clearly because the lights were on. Every time a big wave hit the boat, Uncle Henry held onto whatever was close by. I couldn't make out what he was saying, but he continued to throw the bags of scallops overboard. When he couldn't reach any more bags, I knew he was thinking of unhooking himself. I waved my hands for him to come in. When he saw me, he came and asked me, "What is the matter?"

"You were going to unhook yourself from the cable to reach the rest of the bags."

"What else can I do?" he said.

I handed him some rope and said, "Tie it around your belt, and around the cable, just long enough that you won't be washed overboard. What were you hollering when you were out there?"

"I was counting out loud the money I would have gotten for those scallops that I was throwing overboard.

Frank St. Martin

When we lost a thousand dollars I stopped counting," smirked Uncle Henry.

We all laughed at that one. Uncle Henry went back out and continued throwing bag after bag overboard.

A large wave covered our boat and tossed it sideways toward the next wave that crashed into us. We saw the mast break in two. It came down right where Uncle Henry was standing. I went out the door and grabbed the cable; hand over hand, going toward Uncle Henry. Suddenly, he got up and waved me back to the steering house. Joe grabbed me as I got close to the door. We watched as Uncle Henry continued to throw bags and bags overboard taking a lot of weight off the front of the boat. The lights from the shore became bigger and brighter. We had a long way to go; yet we had a chance.

"I have to lighten the boat more; it's our only chance," I yelled to Uncle Henry. The whole back of the boat was stacked high with bags of scallops.

"No, you're not going out there where there is no cable to attach to!" Uncle Henry said, "I'm the Captain, I give the orders."

"If you go out there, I will go with you," I said.

"No, you won't!" he hollered out to me.

"Uncle Henry," I said, in a calm voice, "We will make land, all three of us, have faith. Don't go out there. If you do, I must go out with you."

Just then a bright light shone on us. Through all the waves and wind, the Coast Guard was talking to us. They told us to head for the bright light on the shore and they would help us to get there. The Coast Guard ship and crew were taking a terrible banging of waves to protect us while we were making headway toward that bright light on the shore. I sent them healing and protection. We could see the bright light and people on shore. The Red Cross was there along with some soldiers.

As we started to get closer to land, Uncle Henry looked at Joe and me and said, "Don't either of you jump off this boat until I give the order!"

"Yes, sir!"

Uncle Henry couldn't control the boat any longer as the large waves pushed us right into the beginning of the dock stretching out into the ocean.

Uncle Henry hollered, "We are going to crash into it! Follow me." We all ran to the front of the boat and jumped on to what remained of the dock where people grabbed us and helped us to safety.

As we sat in chairs with blankets wrapped around us, we watched the BY CRACKY go backward, as it sank. We were told it came on the radio that we were the last ones at sea in the hurricane so the Coast Guard headed out to try to find us, and with a lot of luck, they did. I had a smile on my face, and laughed to myself. I knew they would save us. How else could the three of us have made it back to land?

Joe did not live far from the dock. We shook hands and then he left. Soon everyone was gone. It was about 4 a.m. We had neither money nor clothes. Everything

Frank St. Martin

we had was on the BY CRACKY when it sank. Uncle Henry called my aunt to come and pick us up.

As we rode home, Aunt Lil said, "Frank, your dream came true, didn't it?"

Fifteen

One morning when I was 16 years old, I woke up knowing something was happening to me. I felt as though I was being watched by a classroom of people. My eyes were drawn toward my right side and above me. The classroom of people felt like they were always to the right of me, about twelve feet higher than my eyes. As I meditated on that area, I could see rows of students. Each row was higher than the previous row, and they were all watching. When I opened my eyes it was getting late. I had to get ready for work. I didn't know if I'd had a dream about the young people in a classroom watching me. I hadn't been able to make out any facial features, yet it seemed real. The other feeling I had that day was being in a spotlight about five feet around. When I'd move, it would move.

I did the usual things preparing for work. I got into my car and backed down the very long driveway. I didn't see any cars or trucks yet I knew by the time I got to the end of my driveway I would have to stop and let a black pick-up truck with a red fender on the

The Silent Healer

driver's side pass by. The truck came, and it was exactly as I saw it in my mind, before I saw it with my eyes. I didn't continue backing up at this point. I sat there thinking, *What the heck is the matter with me? How can I see and know what is happening before it actually happens?'* Not knowing the answer, I backed out of the driveway and headed to my job at the shoe factory.

Before I got to the corner I knew that a person across the street would be coming out of his house. He was. It was mind-boggling. I knew everything before I would actually see it. I even knew the number of telephone poles before the next hydrant. I was right. I could do no wrong. This was fun. I even knew what color the first, second and third car would be at the next traffic light, even though the traffic lights were five miles up the road. Why didn't I want to know what color the fourth and fifth car would be? It was because there were no fourth or fifth cars at that traffic light. When I got to the traffic light it was just as I saw it. The colors of the three cars were what I thought they would be.

As I entered this small town, just before the shoe factory, I knew a man would come out of a restaurant, bend down, and pick up a worn out penny. As I got closer to the center of town, yes, there he was, coming out of the restaurant. He looked down on the sidewalk, bent down, and picked up the worn penny. All I had to do was just think, *What's on the sidewalk at the next left going toward the factory?* I would then see everything from the corner all the way to the factory: the children, a woman, men, a dog, a car door opening and a car with its right tire slightly on the sidewalk. *Boy what a gift I have.*

During the day, while at work in the shoe factory, I knew who would be entering the room. I also knew who would be asking me questions and about what. I knew when my cousin was going to come into the room to talk to me. I thought it would be fun to answer his questions before he asked them. I was surprised I couldn't do that. I had to listen to him even though I knew what he was going to ask me. I wasn't allowed to speak.

This game started to have a new twist. I thought I would try this out one more time. A young man with a mustache was going to come into the room and walk up to me at my machine with a pair of shoes. He would want me to put a pair of soles on these shoes, but first he would ask me how long I had been working there. This would be a good test, I thought. When he comes, before he asks, I will answer the questions. I thought his mouth would probably drop open in surprise. His eyes would be big and he wouldn't blink. I saw him as he entered the room and started to walk toward me. I had a big smile on my face. I was ready to answer his questions before he asked them. When he got to my machine he asked me how long I'd been working at the factory. I answered him. I put the soles on the shoes and then he walked away. Now I knew there were some things that I could not do, like answer questions before

The Silent Healer

someone asked.

I wondered what else I could not do. All through the day I knew, before an event would happen, what was going to be the outcome. I was always right. Everything that could possibly occur I would envision before it happened. The fun and games were starting to get to me. I didn't want to know everything before it happened anymore and didn't know how to shut it off.

I knew my boss was going to come into the room and say, "Frank, since you have done plenty of work and are ahead of everyone, you can go home at 2:30 if you wish." Sure enough, he came in and I couldn't even change what I was going to tell him. "Yes, Arthur, thank you. I will go home at 2:30." As I walked through the factory, I knew who was going to say "Hi" to me. I also knew who was going to walk past me, who would cross the aisle, and which car horn was going to toot. This continued all the way home.

I walked into my house about 3:30 locking the door behind me. I was not going out anymore today. I did not want to do this anymore. I felt now that this was torture, and that no one should be able to do this. I started to think about how this all began; remembering how I felt when I woke up in the morning, how all the light was around me, and the feeling that a classroom of people were watching me. I sat up in bed with two pillows behind my neck. I took three deep breaths and slowly counted downward from ten to one. Easily I was in a meditative state of mind and body. No thoughts entered my mind. I had flashes of people, cars and colors, and then it stopped. I felt as though I was on stage, just standing there, with everyone looking at me; but as I looked around all the seats were empty. No one was in this room.

I hollered out, "I don't want to do this anymore!"

I asked God to help me out of this condition. I walked back and forth across the stage, hollering, "Help me God, I don't want to do this anymore!"

Then above me, to the right, I saw the classroom that I remembered seeing in the morning. The students were still looking at me. A teacher or someone who seemed to be in charge entered the room carrying a large book in his hand. All the students looked at him. He pointed his finger at them and then shook his head no. Everyone got out of his or her seat and left. As I looked at the rows of seats, everything disappeared completely.

I got off the bed and stood up, shouting, "I don't want to do this anymore! Please help me, God!"

I made myself something to eat and watched television until 10 p.m. All this time I felt nothing yet had changed. Before I fell asleep I prayed, "Let me go back to the way I was before I started this day of predictions." I meditated again for this curse to leave me. It certainly wasn't a gift that I wanted.

The next morning my alarm clock rang at 5 a.m. I got up and thought, *I'm not going to work today. I'm not going to go through what I went through yesterday.* Suddenly, I felt something had happened. I could feel

The Silent Healer

it, or should I say, I could no longer feel it. The pressure around me from the spotlight was gone. I got dressed, went into my car, drove down the driveway and out to the road. When I got to the intersection there were no cars coming. I felt so happy I could not tell what was happening before it occurred anymore. Never, never, never would I want this to happen to me again!

Sixteen

One day, when I was 16, I drove down to the city to pay my grandparents' electric bill. It was a beautiful day. I parked my car across the street from the Taunton Municipal Light Plant (TMLP).

As I was crossing the street, a young boy I knew approached me and asked me to look at something he had in his bag. It was a baby squirrel. I had never seen a squirrel so small. He said his friend climbed up a tree and took him from the nest. He asked if I would be willing to give him a dollar for it. First, I said I didn't want the squirrel. I told him it is wrong to hurt animals, and he should never do anything like that again.

"I'm sorry," he said, "I will not do it again."

I gave him the dollar then he told me the cloth bag belonged to his mother. I put this tiny squirrel in my front pocket of my pants. When I went in the TMLP and up to the counter to pay the bill, as I did every month, the people behind the counter recognized me and said hello. Suddenly, the squirrel started to dig at my groin. I hollered and bent over, grabbing between my legs, pushing my pants away, carefully, to avoid hurting the squirrel. The people in the office became concerned that I might be having some kind of attack.

"Oh, I just had a sharp pain but it went away," I said.

As I waited for my change and receipt, the squirrel started to dig his way into my groin. I bent over and tried to pull my pants away. By this time, everyone was concerned and someone brought me a chair.

I should have told them the truth but I felt it was too late. I only wanted to leave. I looked at the teller at the window and said, "Could I have my change and receipt please? I think I should hurry and go home."

The tiny squirrel kept digging into me. I couldn't just grab him and pull him out. I thought I would probably kill him or break his leg; he was so tiny and fragile. Finally, with my money and receipt in hand, I was ready to leave, when a caring, young lady brought me a glass of water. I drank the water as quickly as I could, gave the empty glass back, said thank you, and got up to leave.

Just before I got to the door the squirrel scratched me and I bent over and I said, "Oh!"

You could hear everyone sigh as they watched me, bent over, going to the door.

When I got outside, I walked away from the building then slowly, and carefully, took the baby squirrel out of my pocket. It was a slow procedure so I wouldn't hurt him. He kept holding on, every inch of the way out, but I finally got him out of my pant pocket. Afraid I would hurt him if I held him in my hand, I put him in my left shirt pocket and held my shirt away from my body so his toenails wouldn't scratch me. I looked down and saw his little head looking out of my pocket.

I smiled and said, "Everything is okay."

I hurried to my car. Just before I got to the door the squirrel started to claw my left breast. I leaned over the hood of my car and pulled my pocket away from my body. I looked across the street and the people at the TMLP were looking at me. I got in my car and drove away. I never returned to pay the light bill there again. I was so embarrassed that I had been dishonest. Since then, I always mailed the bill with the check enclosed.

When I got home I told my grandparents I wanted to keep the little squirrel. I called him Toby and fed him water and milk with crushed nuts from a little baby doll bottle. He slept in a little basket with a small washcloth covering him. I would put him beside me in the bed so I could keep an eye on him. He grew very fast. Toby became a good friend who would stay on my shoulder as I walked around.

One day Toby jumped off my shoulder and onto the hot stovetop. He squeaked as he jumped around. I quickly pushed him off on to the floor. When I picked him up, he didn't move. It didn't take long for his feet to swell with blisters. He was motionless as I bathed his feet with cool water. I laid him on his back with his feet up and headed to the drugstore. The druggist gave me some pills and a salve to put on his feet to take away the pain.

"If he lives, crush the pills and put the powder in some of his water. It will stop the infection. No charge," he said, "but do not tell anyone I gave these to you."

"Thank you, from both of us!"

Toby would not drink nor eat. He would just lie there. I knew he would die without water so I forced it into him. I also washed his face and paws with cool water and put salve on his feet every day. While I was petting him I would tell him not to die. He would move his head and blink his eyes. He tried to get up, but soon cried out in pain. I sat him up and held him near my body. I walked around with him. I even went outside and walked around the yard to give him some fresh air, hoping this would help him.

He soon started to eat and drink water with no problem. I put the powder in the water and gave it to him each day until the pills were gone. I made little booties for his feet so he wouldn't get an infection when he tried to walk. Toby would try walking and then make a painful noise and fall over on his side. I kept Toby by my side every night. After a week he was walking fairly well and by the second week he was getting back to his old self.

The years went by. Toby and I learned each other's moods and sign language. I could tell if he wanted to eat. He would stand, legs apart, his head going up and down, signaling he wanted food. It was fun learning his ways as he learned mine. In the summer I would take him outside and put him on a branch of our apple

Frank St. Martin

tree. I would then run to the house, open the screen door and tell him to get in. I would look for him, but he was already at my side. He could run faster than I could. When I went to the store he would go with me and wait in the car. When I returned, up on my shoulder he would sit. Even Toby and my dog Skippy got along.

One day, while we were outside playing, a dog came into the yard and ran after Toby who ran into the next yard and up a large tree. He was gone. I couldn't see him anywhere. After the dog left I called for Toby until it was dark outside. No Toby! I left the porch light on in case he tried to return. I was sad that I lost Toby after all these years, but I was happy to think he would be back with his own kind, and would be a happy squirrel.

I woke up at about 5 a.m. hearing something at my bedroom window. I got my flashlight and lifted up my shade and saw Toby hanging on the screen. I went outside and got Toby and brought him into my bedroom. He jumped on the bed and under the blanket as he now slept near my feet at night. My feet were cold so I put on a pair of woolen stockings and went to sleep. When I woke up, I lay there looking at where Toby was sleeping, a lump under the blanket. I rubbed my feet together, touching skin on skin. How could this be since I had put on woolen socks? I looked under the blankets and couldn't believe what I saw. There lay Toby, rolled up like a ball, on top of a pile of wool yarn. No stockings were on my feet but I had no cuts or marks either. He unwound all my stockings without waking me. This was hard to believe but there he was lying on the evidence. I patted him and laughed. He looked up at me and I patted him some more.

I prepared his food of nuts and grains and sometimes a piece of bread. I watched him eat, but something was wrong. I could feel it. The way he looked at me was different. Between eating Toby would run to the window and look out. He never did that before. After I ate, with Toby on my shoulder, I went outside into the yard. Toby jumped down and ran out of the yard and up another tree. I watched as he jumped from limb to limb. I called him, but he never looked back at me. I stayed home all day, looking in the trees. I saw him a couple of times sitting on a limb. It looked like he was eating something. I called him, but he would disappear in the branches. When it started to get dark I put the porch light on. I went outside and called Toby one more time. When I entered the house, Toby entered with me. I was so happy. I patted him, but he didn't feel right. The softness of his skin was not there. He was tense.

Toby went into another room where I had a large cage for him to go in and out whenever he felt like it. It had no door. I had taken it off years before. His water and food were always there. He jumped up, entered the cage and just lay there. I went to pat him and he chattered his teeth at me; something he had never done before. I went to bed without Toby for the first time. In the morning I got up to see if Toby was all right. Toby was dead. I cried. I made a wooden box and buried him wrapped in the small washcloth. I lost a special friend.

Seventeen

At the age of 18, I signed up for the Navy for four years. I traveled to many beautiful places around the world, met interesting people, and held a variety of jobs on the ship including being head cook for the Chiefs Quarters.

I remember the beautiful weather on the day the ship docked in Nice, France. As I waited in line, ready to go ashore, I wondered where the churches were. Would there be any entertainment to be found? A few of my friends and I decided to stay together. Once ashore, we visited bar after bar. Although I didn't drink much, it was fun because at every bar there was always something happening. People were singing and dancing. The music was wonderful and the ladies were beautiful.

As we walked down the streets looking for different places to visit, I saw a large beautiful church that I wanted to go into. The rest of my friends had other things on their minds. They weren't too enthusiastic about going into a church. We parted for the time being.

The Silent Healer

I told them I would meet them later in one of the places on the main street. I entered the church and sat close to the altar. Everything was so beautiful. I lost myself in prayer until a priest asked if he could be of any help. I looked at my watch; an hour and a half had passed by. I thanked the priest and left the church. I decided to go window shopping. I purchased many nice things that I would send home to my grandparents, other relatives and friends.

When I returned to the ship, I saw a sign posted. It read: "Experienced cook wanted. Apply at the Chefs' Quarters." I thought this had to be better than my current job of washing the decks and painting walls. I was not the best cook, but I was sure I could learn fast. I went to the bookstore and bought a book on cooking short order meals, fancy dishes and salads. When I got on the ship I went straight to the Chefs' Quarters and inquired about the job.

One question was asked, "Do you cook with flavor?"

"Of course, that's how I like my own food."

I had the job! I would start when the ship left port. I was told I had to pick three mess cooks to work under my supervision (I liked that). I also would be sleeping in a different area of the ship; just for cooks. My experience so far was in cooking bacon, eggs and opening cans of soup to which I added flavor, salt and pepper. I was pretty limited but felt, with a cookbook, I could do a great job. I opened my bag, put the book on the table and looked at the cover. "Oh no," I said, as I looked at its pages. Everything was in French!

Frank St. Martin

When I arrived at the bookstore counter the sales lady said, "You have the wrong book, right? I put aside a book for you in English; I knew you would be back."

I thought one day I could look back on my service records, relive the memories, and possibly write an entire book about the wonderful events I had encountered in the Navy. There is much to be told about my being involved and helping others during that time. I will always be proud that I served in the U.S. Navy.

Eighteen

When I came home from the Navy I was 22 years old. My grandfather was very sick. I was home just one day when he passed away.

His last words to me were, "I enjoyed having you as a son. Take care of your grandmother."

He then closed his eyes and passed on to a better life.

I really liked being in the service so I was planning to sign up for another four years in the Navy. After my grandfather passed away, all my aunts and uncles got together at the small house where I was born and raised. I heard them talking that they could not help take care of their mother since they were married and busy with their lives. The best place, they all agreed, was a nursing home about 15 miles away. They talked about how much money they would get when they sold the house, and they wouldn't have to feel guilty not visiting her since it was so far away.

When I heard this, I thought, *My grandmother wasn't ready for a nursing home. She did all the cleaning and cooking and was still very active.*

The Silent Healer

I changed my mind about the Navy. My responsibility was to my grandmother, first, and I would be there to help her. She had diabetes so I asked a nurse to show me how to administer the needle with insulin so that I could give it to her if she couldn't do it herself. I asked Meme every day what she would like to eat. I would make it in the morning before I went to work and put it in the refrigerator so all she would have to do was to warm it.

She was capable of cooking, but I felt I owed it to her. I went to work and then came home and never went out without taking my grandmother with me. We went out to restaurants. I took her on a trip to Florida. We had a good life. Every time I would ask her if she wanted to go out, it didn't matter where we were going, her answer was always yes.

I had no friends, only my co-workers at my job in the shoe factory. My uncles and aunts very seldom came to the house. When they did it was always for a very, very short visit.

Three years went by and one day, at the age of 79, my grandmother knew she was dying. She asked for her oldest son, Freddy. I called him and told him his mother wanted to talk to him now.

While he was in the bedroom talking to her, I heard her say, "Make sure that Frank has the house. He has been so good to your father and me."

My Uncle Freddy said, "I promise," and within an hour she passed away.

The next day all my aunts and uncles came to the house while my grandmother lay in a funeral home. They fought over the furniture and everything else they could put in their cars: tables, chairs, knickknacks, pictures, blankets and on and on they broke the closet door that had a lock on it instead of asking me for the key. They took everything of value including thousands of dollars that I had earned and saved each week. They fought among themselves about who would get what.

One of my uncles said, "This is my mother's house. You are nothing to us."

He told me that he and his wife were going to sleep in my bed that night. My other uncles and aunts just looked on, as though nothing were happening. I slept in a motel that night, or should I say, I sat up thinking and weeping. In the days that followed mostly everything, including my tools, was taken. The house was given to me. I had a place to live, thanks to my grandmother. The value of the house was $3000 in 1956. Only one uncle and aunt were honorable. They took nothing even though they were poor, Raymond and Eva St. Martin. Their names are worth mentioning.

As my aunts and uncles grew old and rich, before they passed on, every one of them called me, crying, and said they were sorry for what they had done to me and asked for forgiveness.

I said to each one, "Yes, I forgive you." And I meant it.

The years went by and I continued my healing in silence. I had a new car and lady friends. I appreciated my past but now it was my time for fun and life was enjoyable. I worked hard and spent my money on nice things including a motorcycle. I drove fast and took chances, but no one ever got hurt around me. I enjoyed all the challenges and excitement as I lived through these happy times. The fun I was having slowed down considerably as more and more people heard of my services and came to me for healing. I liked having fun, but I mostly enjoyed sharing my gift of healing through God.

Nineteen

One day, as I was leaving the house for church, my father drove into the driveway and told me he was living nearby. As we talked, he said he went to a local restaurant each afternoon. I told him I would meet him there occasionally. Well, I did meet him, almost every day, and had coffee or a meal together. He still talked about my name being St. Martin. After a few months, I thought I would please my father by changing my name to Bento, Jr., which is all he ever asked of me. (I never would have changed my name if my grandparents were still alive.) I hired a lawyer, went to court, and told the judge why I wanted to change my name.

He agreed and said, "I give you permission to change your name to Frank Bento, Jr. as of now."

I was very pleased with myself. After all these years my father was going to get his wish, or so I thought.

I went to my father's house and told him that I had changed my name to "Frank Bento, Jr." He looked pleased, but told me he was going to look into it further.

The next day when I met him at the restaurant he said, "You only have permission to use the name Bento, Jr."

I replied "Yes, this is what the judge said; my name is now Bento, Jr."

I'll never forget what he said to me next. "I showed those St. Martin's! I told them I would have you change your name!"

This is not what I expected from him. I really thought he would be pleased. Nothing changed, only my name, and all the paperwork that went with it. He still treated me as an outsider. I was so disappointed. I didn't know what to do next.

My father had re-married and divorced since my mother passed away. I had met his wife so I decided to talk to her about my father.

She told me, "He is a good man, and has helped a lot of people. Your father loves you. He always talked about you with love and affection."

I told her about my name change and how I thought that would please him. "He's pleased," she said, "When you get to know him, you will see."

I very seldom saw him anymore. He travelled back and forth to California.

One day I received a phone call from someone telling me that my father fell and was sick and needed my help. I was told where he lived and went to his apartment. I found him looking older with a head wound. He told me he didn't know what happened. All he said was, "I just fell down and when I got up I noticed my head was bleeding."

I washed the cut and put a bandage on it. He said he felt better and wanted to go get a coffee. I went with him and, as the day progressed, he looked better. I brought him back to his apartment and said I would see him the next day. I watched him as he started to climb the stairs to his apartment. About four stairs up his knee gave way. He held onto the railing until I helped him, and then he sat down on the stairs. I told him I would bring him either to the hospital or to my house, whichever way he preferred. He chose to go to my house. I gathered his clothes and drove him to my home. I gave him his own bedroom.

At about 5:30 a.m. the next morning, I woke my father up and told him I was going to work and that I would arrange for someone to stay with him during the day and prepare meals for him.

Weeks went by and everything seemed fine. My father looked good and healthy. I told him he could stay with me for as long as he wanted.

A few weeks later I received a call at work from the woman caring for my father telling me he was not there. I went home right away to find my father and his clothes gone. I went down to the city and stopped by the barbershop where my father would often frequent. I asked a man there if he had seen my father. "Yes," he said. "He was here early this morning and when he left he was going to his new apartment in the same building where he used to live." I went to see him and asked him why he didn't tell me he was leaving.

"I don't have to tell you anything! I can do what I want to do!"

I told him that I assumed he could, but out of decency, he could have told me or his caregiver he was leaving. I didn't want to argue with him. I knew he felt better, and he was very independent. I told him I would bring him something to eat every morning and afternoon.

"Ok, if you want to," he said. I left and went back to work.

Every morning I brought breakfast to my father and every noon left him a full meal. I varied the menu every day for him.

After about four weeks I asked him, "Are you feeling okay?"

"Yes," he replied.

I told him I would stop by Sunday and take him out for a ride.

"No," he said, as he did many times before. "I have someone taking me out for a ride."

I asked if he needed some money. "No," he said. "I think I'll go to sleep now, for a while."

I was there about ten minutes then left. Monday through Saturday I supplied his meals. "On Sunday," he said, "don't bring me anything to eat."

On Monday I brought my father his meal, and we had the usual short conversation. I walked down the hallway. A door opened and a man asked if he could talk with me. He left the door open and I walked into his apartment. I followed him with caution. I wondered why he wanted to talk to me in his apartment. He asked if the man I was bringing food to was my father.

"Yes," I said.

"He throws all the food you bring to him away."

"What?" I replied, as I felt the hurt go through my body and heart. I became weak and sat down. I thought of all the months I went out of my way to please him by delivering food every morning and afternoon.

"Are you sure?" I asked.

"Yes," he said. "He puts the food you bring him in a plastic bag and about 1 o'clock every day he dumps it into the rubbish container. Please don't tell your father that I told you. I don't want any problems." I assured him I wouldn't tell him.

I went back to my father's apartment. I knocked on the door. He opened it and was surprised to see me. I saw a plastic bag in his hand. I grabbed it away from him and looked in the bag. It was true, his breakfast and the meal I just brought him were in the large plastic bag, ready to be thrown away. I asked him why he was doing this!

"I don't want anything from a St. Martin!" he replied abruptly. Even though my name was changed to Bento, Jr., he still only remembered all the years my name was St. Martin. I told him I was his son first, how I cared about him and made sure he had good food to eat.

"I don't care. I don't want anything from you." We just looked at each other.

"Call me when you need me," I said. I left with a lot of sorrow and hurt. He could not get over seeing me as part of the St. Martin family. Despite all my time and trouble, he apparently preferred getting his food from the diner across the street.

One day I received a phone call from someone saying that my father was at the bottom of the stairs and could not get up. I rushed to his apartment, and there he was sitting on the floor. I talked to him and asked if he wanted me to help him up.

"Yes, I've been here all night and no one saw me. I can't get up."

I helped him up and walked him to my car and drove him to the hospital. I was told he had a stroke and needed 24-hour care. He was sent to a nearby nursing home where I visited him 3 to 4 times a week. After a few weeks he started to feel better. He started talking about leaving and returning to his apartment. He was walking and talking well. A few days later I received a call that he had fallen and went into a coma. I thought this might happen. He never recovered.

At his funeral, I thought there might be a few people that would come to see him. What a surprise. At the wake, the line of people went out the funeral home door and down the sidewalk. Everyone knew him. They all told me stories of what a good person he was and how he helped others who couldn't afford food.

"Your father was there every week with food for my family," one man said. "When I was working, I wanted to pay your father back for all the weeks he supplied us with food. Your father said to me, 'If you know of someone else who needs food, help him.' So I did. I could never thank your father enough."

The tears came to my eyes as people told me about my father and how much he had helped them. I listened to all the good things my father had done in his lifetime. I wished we had known each other better, and that he would have really thought of me as his son. After my father passed on, I changed my name back to Frank St. Martin.

Twenty

In the previous chapters I have attempted to illustrate how meaningful it has been to be blessed with the ability to help others using spiritual healing through God. I have been very interested throughout my life in exploring healing energy methodologies. I was in my sixties when I had my first exposure to Reiki.

On one hot day, I decided to take a ride to the beach and just relax for a couple of hours. On my way home, I stopped at a bookstore and spent a lot of time looking at healing books. Most of the books I already owned, and the others were not what I wanted.

As I started to leave, I noticed a book that had just fallen to the floor from a shelf. No one was near it when it fell so I walked up the aisle, picked up the book, and put it back on the shelf. I looked at the cover and noticed it was about healing with Reiki. I opened the book and scanned its contents. I thought what an unusual thing to happen; a book that was in the wrong aisle and wrong section, fell to the floor just at the time

I passed by. I bought the book then sat in my car and started reading.

Reiki is a hands-on healing technique used by a practitioner who is a vehicle through which the energy is transmitted to another person to relieve discomfort, reduce stress and promote relaxation. When I got home I continued reading and decided I had to learn this technique. I found a course and enrolled to become a Reiki Master.

Little did I know that the last day in becoming a Reiki Master would be a day I would never forget. There were ten students including myself who were learning to channel healing energy through our minds, our bodies, and out our hands. Our teacher, a Reiki Master who had come from India and had been teaching for 20 years, was excellent. He paid attention to each one of us, to make sure that everyone was learning correctly.

The Reiki teacher told us to do all of the procedures alone even though we were learning as a group. This was a crash course in learning Reiki I, Reiki II, and we were to master it within five days. After each day of class, which was eight or nine hours, we were given homework to do for the following day.

Many nights I would be up until 2 a.m. studying. The class started at 9 a.m. and we were tested each day on our homework. In addition to all the assigned lessons, each day I studied far beyond what was required to learn more. All my spare time was devoted to studying. I didn't want simply to be called a Reiki

Master, I wanted to be the best; only then would I feel worthy to help others.

As the days went by, we felt good that we were learning and that our teacher knew what he was doing. We were all working as a team and, individually, we helped each other. On the last day of our class we went through some rituals. The teacher dimmed the lights and told us to relax and close our eyes. After a few minutes of deep breathing exercises, we all sat quietly. No sounds could be heard.

Then the teacher said, "Listen only to me, quiet your mind. I will lead you to a place where you will meet your Reiki Master. He will be with you and help you whenever you need him."

He took us on a journey to a wide hallway with windows on our left and seven doors on our right. As each one of us, alone, entered the large hallway with windows and seven doors, we were told only one door would open to each one of us. "Behind the door, you will meet your Reiki Master. You will talk to him and receive him as your friend and a helper for life." We all talked to our Reiki Master.

Then our teacher said, "Open your eyes and know that you are sitting here in class. After a while, we all started to talk to each other with excitement in our voices, sharing our experiences about meeting our Reiki Masters.

The lights in the room were turned up bright, and our teacher questioned each one of us:

"Did we meet our Reiki Master?"

"Were we satisfied?"

Every one answered, "Yes!"

Being so late in the day, he suggested that we all come back the next morning to tell our story of what happened. He also said every one passed. Tomorrow he would announce that everyone is a Reiki Master. We were all very excited as we went our separate ways.

I was so excited about what had happened to me as I approached the hallway with windows and the seven doors. I will never forget this to my dying day.

I drove back to the hotel and called a lady friend and shared with her what had happened. My Reiki Master, who spoke to me would be forever with me. Through the night his words rang in my ears and the vibrations went through my body.

The next morning I drove back to the classroom. Everyone was outside talking about their Reiki Master until the doors of the building were opened. When anyone asked me what happened when I saw my Reiki Master, I replied, "I will only tell my story in class."

When we all went inside the classroom our teacher said, "I'm sure we're going to hear some exciting stories from everyone."

After we all sat down in a circle, the teacher said, "Let's start with Frank on my right side and work around to hear everyone's journey in meeting their Reiki Master."

I asked if I could be last to tell my story. "It is so special, I believe, it deserves to be told last."

The teacher looked at me and said, "Yes, I believe it should be told last. I have noticed there is something about you, Frank, that you have a special gift. I am sure you will have a special Reiki Master to help you."

Next to me was a nurse who started to tell her story.

I didn't sleep all night. What a wonderful experience I had meeting my Reiki Master. I was in a hallway with windows on the left and seven doors on the right. I walked up to a door and said, "Is my Reiki Master in here?" The door did not open so I went to the next door and asked, "Is my Reiki Master in here?" After I approached a few more doors, asking and wondering, I began to question whether there would be any door for me. At the sixth door I asked, "Is my Reiki Master in here?" The door opened slowly and there, sitting in a brightly lit room, was my Reiki Master. The back of this room was half round, and beautiful colored draperies covered the wall. Long thin tables were close to the outside walls. On the tables there was an assortment of different items, all in gold. Behind the tables were gold statues with life like features. The eyes of the statues seemed to follow me as I entered more of the room. Beautiful colored vases and gold statues were on each side of my Reiki Master. As I looked at him I noticed his legs were crossed in a lotus position. The amazing thing was that he was floating about twelve inches above the pillows he had been sitting on. I asked, "Are you my

Reiki Master who will always be by my side to help me when I need you?"

"Yes," *he replied in a clear loving voice. "I will always be close. You can call me at any time and I will come and help you."*

"Thank you."

I turned and walked out of the room into the hallway. The next thing I remembered was opening my eyes and sitting here in class.

Everyone in class listened to her story and understood her excitement and pleasure. Each person in the group had a slightly different encounter in meeting their Reiki Master. Some spoke slowly, others rapidly. Some Reiki Masters were tall, others short, with varying strengths. Everyone had their own special Reiki Master to call on anytime they needed help. What a wonderful feeling to know that you have a lifelong friend; a Reiki Master whom you can call upon at any time to help you.

Before I started to share my experience, the instructor suggested that we resume after lunch.

I noticed that everyone was unusually quiet. I asked our instructor if he noticed this also.

"Yes," he said, "Everyone was remembering their internal dream of this great event that had happened in their life."

Looking at me he asked, "Are you a healer?"

"Yes."

"I thought so. I could tell by the way everyone was drawn to you, always trying to help you."

Frank St. Martin

When we got back from lunch everyone sat quietly and listened as I told my story. I looked around and noticed the all the participants were leaning toward me, sitting at the edge of their seats, waiting for me to speak.

This is my true story of what happened to me as I was united with my Reiki Master, who has been with me and will always be with me. I entered this wide hallway with large windows, on my left and on my right were seven doors. I knew, behind one of these doors was my Reiki Master. I looked around the room noticing the high ceilings that were as white as snow. The walls were pale yellow and gold. The carpet had markings with beautiful light shades of color. I looked out the windows to see trees with green and brown leaves, and trees with shades of yellow and red leaves. There were large pine trees; some had berries growing on them. On the sides of the cement path were small red and orange bushes. As I continued down the hallway, I could see through the windows the scenery changing to green grass and beautiful colorful flowers. A small breeze moved the cluster of flowers like small waves in the ocean.

It was now time to meet my Reiki Master. I stood, looking at the seven doors in front of me. I knew only one door would open for me. What door would it be? The answer came to me. I counted three doors from my left, then three doors from my right. The seventh door in the middle was mine and opened as I asked, "Is my Reiki Master in here?" Suddenly the width and the length of the door expanded, pushing the walls and the ceiling away to make room for its increasing size. When the doorway expanded, it sounded like a rumble of thunder as it moved wider and higher. I stood there without moving, noticing that no wall or ceiling material fell to the floor. The door in front of me was about twenty feet high and eight feet wide. It opened toward me to the right.

Inside the doorway, there was a giant of a man with a sword standing on my right. His hand rested on the handle, while the point of the sword touched the floor. As I entered the room and slowly passed by this giant, I noticed I was only as tall as his knees. I felt he would not harm me. He could have done this at any time if he wanted. I believed he must be here to protect this entrance to allow only the person who was supposed to be here to enter. I walked further into the room and noticed the designs on the walls. There were Egyptian pictures and symbols on the walls like those I had seen in the movies. I looked at the ceiling, which was also painted with pictures. At the end of this long room was a door of regular size. There were no windows or light fixtures in this room. Yet the room was well lit. As I walked toward the door I could feel the excitement and love coming into my heart. Behind this door was where I would meet my Reiki Master. I was told once we meet, we are forever bonded to one another.

I need this Reiki energy in my life, I thought, so that this will be another healing method I can use to help more people. I felt good just thinking of this. As I approached the door, it opened. I entered into a dark room. Looking deep inside the room, about eye level was a beam of light, or electricity, going back and forth. From end to end it was about thirty inches wide. I could feel a vibration in the air as this beam of light continued with a humming sound.

Not seeing my Reiki Master, I asked, "Who are you?"

From the light source a voice said, "You know who I am!"

While I was standing at this location, I felt as though many eyes were watching me. It also felt like a holy place, but I could only see this spark of light going back and forth in front of me in this dark room.

I did something foolish; I walked quickly toward the moving spark of light and hollered, "Who are you?"

The voice came back at me like a thundering vibration hitting me. I quickly fell backward and down to the floor. The voice clearly and very loudly said, "You know who I am!"

In a panicked voice I said, "Yes, I know!"

I got up and bowed to the moving light source and thanked it. I thanked it again for allowing me to be here. I felt humble and full of love. I was not afraid. I bowed and backed out of the room while watching the light go back and forth. Before turning away from the room I said thank you one more time. I walked back to the large doorway, which was still open. The giant guardian observed me and protected the entrance as I walked out across the hall and stood next to the windows. When I looked back, the large door was gone and in its place was a normal size door. All I remember was opening my eyes and being in the classroom at that point.

When I finished my story I asked the class, "Did anyone go through the center door?"

Not one classmate said yes. Everyone was astonished to hear my story.

The teacher said to me, "Never, in all my years of teaching, have I encountered such a story. In India, you would be considered a Holy Man."

As we departed we shook hands and hugged each other. We walked away with a spiritual healing gift, a friend and Reiki Master to call upon when needed. I sat in my car and waited until everyone had departed. I then drove toward home to enjoy my life just as I always have. I have always known I was not alone.

Twenty-One

One Saturday morning I didn't have anything planned so I decided to devote the day to writing. I wanted to write a memoir sharing some of my spiritual healing experiences that were so extraordinary and had such a profound impact on my life and others. I sat at my desk at 9 a.m. and was ready to begin on my book when the phone rang. It was a lady who wanted an estimate on painting her house. The quiver in her voice made it sound like an emergency, and that she wanted it done now. She gave me her address and I left right away to see her. When I drove into her driveway, I noticed it was a large beautiful home and that it didn't really need painting.

I met Kathy who told me that she, her husband and children had lived there only a few months. She said she did not like the color of the house. I gave her my price. She accepted it and wanted me to start right away.

One week later I started to paint her house and completed it twelve days later. It looked much better in beige than the previous color brown. When she paid me, she commented that she hoped now that her luck would change. I was surprised that she would think that and asked her if her luck had been bad. She told me that her house had been broken into twice, which according to her neighbors had not happened before in that neighborhood. Kathy told me, as she looked down at the ground, from the time they'd moved in she felt like someone was watching her. She wanted to move but her husband and children liked the house and neighborhood.

"If I continue to complain," she said, "I know my husband will sell this house. It is a nice neighborhood and this house is everything I want, but the feeling of being watched all the time while I'm home is getting to me."

"Often when I put things down then return to get them they have moved to another location. I know it sounds crazy and, I have reasoned with myself, that it isn't possible. Before I called you to paint my house, I was going to walk around in the backyard. I didn't go very far when I had the feeling that something was going to happen to me and I ran back into the house.

"The day I called you, I thought, *I'm going to walk in my backyard.* As I started my walk, I immediately felt that someone was watching me. The tree in front of me started to shake. I ran quickly into my house and locked the door. I looked out the kitchen window and wondered if the wind could have caused it to shake. *Anything is possible*, I thought as I looked for an answer, *yet today is very calm, no wind.*"

Frank St. Martin

Kathy told me she looked out her kitchen window again and the tree started to bend toward her. About two feet above the ground, the tree snapped and the limbs hit the kitchen window as it came crashing down to the ground.

She called a tree surgeon who could not tell her the reason why the tree broke off at about two feet above the ground. He also didn't know why a tree that is naturally tilted away from the house would fall toward the kitchen window. He said he had never seen anything like it before.

After hearing her story, I told Kathy I could help her. She hired me right away when I told her I could rid her house and yard of anything evil. When I arrived the next day, I carried a lantern with a candle lit inside of it. I told Kathy I was going to begin around the outside and then come into the house and bless and clear every room with God, in my mind, as my protector.

I also told Kathy, whatever she might see outside while I'm out there, she was to stay in the house. She agreed.

I started to walk into the backyard making the sign of the cross. I felt a sensation that I was now being watched and a powerful energy field was pushing me. It felt like my whole body was being squeezed and it was getting hard to breathe. I started to walk across the backyard and when I looked down to the ground, I saw the dirt forming a circle around me. I didn't move. I just looked at what was happening. The dirt seemed alive as it moved and started to swirl around me, counter clockwise. The dirt came up to my knees, circling around me, and then moved higher and higher.

Kathy opened the kitchen window, as she looked at the dirt circling around me. She hollered, "Run, Frank," over and over. She was really frightened.

"Kathy, shut the window," I yelled back.

She stopped yelling, backed away from the window, and stood there watching.

The dirt continued to swirl around me. The lantern was still lit. I continued to make the sign of the cross in the air. With God in my mind as my protector, I was not afraid. I suddenly realized that I was standing there unable to walk. It was like I was hypnotized and I was waiting for something to happen to me. My legs felt heavy and numb. I forced each foot forward, one in front of the other. I walked slowly toward a large tree. The dirt still encircled me and by now it was almost to my shoulder height. Once I was next to the tree I put my arms out and hugged the tree. I asked for wisdom and strength. The swirling dirt stopped and made a small hill of dirt around me. The energy field that seemed to push against me disappeared. Everything was back to normal.

"Frank," Kathy called to me, "You'd better come into the house. The door is unlocked."

"Kathy, please close the window. I cannot be harmed. I will be all right."

I started again to walk across the backyard. I was about twenty feet away from the tree and, again, the dirt started swirling around me. This time it was coming up toward my shoulders much faster than before. I turned around in this circle of dirt, hollering loudly, "Can you hear me," I said. "Are you afraid to face me? Are you hiding behind this circle of dirt because you're afraid to face me? You coward, you!"

I quickly walked to another tree and repeated the same things as I did before. The circle of dirt stopped. I yelled again, "Are you afraid of me? God is with me. Are you afraid? Is that why you must hide?"

I looked at the kitchen window and there was Kathy waving her hands for me to come into the house. I knew I would never leave this yard until I had complete control over this dirt that encircled me, and no longer felt that someone was watching me. I wondered what would happen if the dirt went over my head. Would I be able to breathe?

As I walked away from this tree the dirt started swirling again about ankle high, and then quickly rose to my knees. The dirt was circling me faster like it was angry with me. It took a lot of my strength to overcome this pushing and pulling. I had a strong feeling someone was intensely looking at me. I looked around. I could see Kathy was still at the open window. I looked up at the top of a row of pine trees. There was a black cloud, about twenty feet wide and five feet high and about eight feet apart were two slanting eyes looking at me. I started to walk and I noticed the eyes were following me. I held up my lantern and continuously made the sign of the cross toward the eyes. I yelled as I walked toward the staring eyes.

"In the name of God, leave this place. I command you to leave!"

In the background I could hear Kathy yelling for me to run or to come into the house. All she could see was that the dirt was up to my shoulders. I noticed as the dirt circled me above my shoulders, I had to take deeper breaths to get any air. With the lit lantern, I reached out toward the staring eyes repeatedly making the sign of the cross.

Looking up at the eyes and the black cloud, I hollered, "I will never stop praying to God to eliminate you!"

I continued to pray out loud and used God's name as my protector. Then everything stopped; the wind, the spinning dirt around me, the pressure on my body, the feeling of being watched. The black cloud vanished. I hollered to Kathy, who was extremely frightened by now, "Everything is all right. I will be in the house soon."

I continued around the house without incident. I walked across the backyard one more time just to make sure that everything was all right.

I went into the house and with Kathy by my side, proceeded to each room and closet. Every door was opened. I did my best to eliminate evil and bring peace and harmony into the house. When I was done, I sat with Kathy and had a cup of tea. I thought it was necessary to make sure Kathy was calm, and that she knew she would not have any further problems. When I left the house, Kathy thanked me over and over again. With a smile I said, "Your welcome."

As I drove out the driveway, I thought, *Never again will she have a problem with evil manifesting in her yard or house.* I drove toward home believing I'd probably never see Kathy again.

When I arrived home, my lady friend Andi said, "I could go for a coffee and a muffin, how about you?"

Once we were in the coffee shop I started to tell her what had happened. As I looked at her, I thought, *I don't think she believes me.* I was going to end the story by saying everything turned out all right when I noticed Kathy was coming into the coffee shop. She saw my car as she was driving by and had to stop and tell me everything was still fine. She'd walked across the backyard and no one seemed to be looking at her anymore. Kathy started from the beginning and told Andi what had just happened at her house. When she was done she thanked me again and left.

Andi asked if I had been afraid.

"No. I was protected."

Twenty-Two

Many years ago people used to be afraid of anyone who had the ability to heal. It was frequently looked upon as the power of evil. This is why I, as well as others, had a hard time using the gift of healing when trying to help people. The biggest lesson I learned was to be silent. When you helped someone in a healing you were called a witch or a warlock. At a young age it not only hurt, it was scary. It helped me to remember what my grandmother always said to me: Be the silent healer; and that's who I became. As an open channel to healing, energy flows in and through me to whomever I see or think of as I present this healing to them.

One day, I really felt like going to a healing seminar, but I hadn't found any advertisement on healing that had captured my interest. Looking out my window I saw the mailman leaving and as I sorted out my mail, there it was: an invitation to a seminar on healing in New York State. It was about two hundred miles away, but I didn't care how far it was.

Day one of the seminar was interesting. I introduced myself to everyone there. It didn't take long to realize that they all knew one another, except me. The gentleman who led the seminar was very knowledgeable and presented his views clearly. I observed as healing demonstrations were performed in the group. The afternoon went by with more instruction. It became clear that for much more money, one could go to their main company and learn considerably more about healing.

The second day I arrived at 7:30 a.m. and was told we would end the day at around 6 or 7 p.m. I looked forward to a long enjoyable day. After more information on healing was presented to us, a demonstration of healing was to be given to a man who was an invited guest. He told us a story of what happened to him many years earlier while changing a flat tire. He was kneeling down on the driver's side to take the tire off when a car ran into him. The driver stopped, walked over, looked at him and then drove away. That's all he remembered as he lay there with broken bones and bleeding. He woke up in a hospital on the critical list. He had a head injury, fractured legs, broken ribs and shattered bones. He had to learn how to walk again. The police never found out who hit him and left him there to die.

He told us, "I have days with pain; my right knee gives me the most discomfort. You would think I was a strong healthy person."

Looking at him, we all agreed. The gentleman lay down on a thick blanket on the floor, and then indicated to the instructor every place he had pain. He reiterated that his right knee gave him the most distress. The instructor told this man to close his eyes and relax as he lay down on the blanket. He then called out three students' names and directed them to the left side of this man; one at the foot, another by the hip, and the third at the shoulder. Then he called two more names; placed one student by the man's right hip and the other at his right shoulder. As everyone watched the instructor, he looked at all of us, and then asked me,

"What's your name?"

"Frank St. Martin."

"I want you to do the healing on his right knee, down to his foot." The instructor and the rest of the students were smiling because they knew this was the most difficult area of this man's body in need of healing. I smiled because I knew this is where the gentleman hurt the most.

We were to spend an hour performing the healing. All eyes were watching me as I knelt on the floor next to the right knee and foot of the gentleman. The other five healers had their eyes closed part of the time. They were busy with their hand and face movements.

I brought my two hands together, palms up, in front of me. I waited for a long time, centering myself, for the healing vibrations to begin. When I felt the surge of energy flowing around inside me, I put my right hand on his foot and my left hand on his knee, and then closed my eyes. I moved my hand in a one-stroke

The Silent Healer

fashion from the top of the man's knee down and out through his ankle. As I continued this motion, within a couple of minutes, the man started wiggling. With his eyes still closed he kept moving his leg back and forth. The instructor asked if he was all right.

"Yes," he answered.

I concentrated on the pain being removed and for the healing energy to work for his highest good. In a few minutes his body, arms and legs shook, and then stopped.

The instructor told us the hour was almost up. My knee hurt from being in the same position for so long. I could feel my knee as well as the gentleman's knee drawing energy from me. I had an endless supply of healing energy to give.

When the hour was finished, the instructor said, "All healers get up and join me over here."

The gentleman got up, moved around and thanked all of us for working on him. He said he felt better now than he had when he first arrived. We were all surprised when he asked who worked on his right knee. Everyone stepped aside and looked at me. None of us knew what to expect.

The instructor said, "Frank, you did his right knee, correct?"

"Yes, I did."

As I looked at this man, I saw no expression on his face to indicate his concern. He came to me and put his hands on my shoulders. I looked up at him and saw he had a big smile on his face.

"You are a good healer," he said. "I could feel the heat and vibrations from your hands around my knee all the way down to my foot. I have no pain! The pain, for the first time, is gone!"

He then shook my hand and said, "Thank you."

He looked at the instructor and said, "I want to thank you for inviting me here today. This is the first time the pain in my knee has stopped."

The instructor asked him to come outside on the porch and speak with him. No sooner had the instructor and the gentleman left the room, everyone gathered around me. The questions began. "What is your name?" "Where are you from?" "How long have you been a healer?"

I replied that the healing success was not solely due to my efforts, but was a result of everyone's contribution.

The instructor then came into the room and asked to speak with me. Once we were outside, he asked me if I would come to work for him.

"You would have to come to California. We will teach you what we do, and you can teach us what you do. I will pay you well," he said.

I told him that it was an honor to be asked to work for him and his large company. However at this time in my life, being in my sixties I would not be willing to move to another state. He offered me good money to change my mind.

I shook his hand and said, "No."

After lunch, we were told to go upstairs. We were going to work on a young lady, Mary, one of the healers in our group sessions who had serious problems. Upstairs, in a small bedroom, she laid down on her back with a pillow under her head.

The instructor asked, "When you are comfortable, tell us what problems you have."

She told us she had family problems, business difficulties, tension and fear, and physical pain in her arms and legs.

"My biggest problem is my eyes. I cannot produce tears. It has become a serious medical issue."

The instructor selected five people and assigned three of them on her right side and two of them on her left side. We all knew there was one person missing. Who would be designated to work on her eyes?

When everyone assumed their respective positions, the instructor looked at me and said, "You take her eyes."

"Thank you," I said as I put my hands across her eyes.

As I prayed and visualized her eyes shedding tears, I could see actual tears coming down her face. For a very long time I continued to visualize tears coming from her eyes. Eventually a big smile appeared on her face as she yelled, "I'm crying!"

I don't know how much time had elapsed when Mary opened her eyes and gleefully exclaimed, "I'm crying!" as the happy tears rolled down her face. "I'm crying, I'm crying!"

Mary asked if she could use a phone to call her doctor and tell him the good news. We all listened as she told her doctor her crying produced an abundance of tears.

She came over to me and gave me a big hug and a kiss on the cheek, and said, "Thank you very much."

We took a half hour break and I sat outside on the porch where a lady who was part of the group approached me.

"I have a business proposal to offer you. I have two offices in New York. I do healing three days in one office and three days in the other office. I would be willing to accept you as a full partner, fifty/fifty split after bills are paid."

I thanked her for considering me, but told her I would not move to New York.

A couple named Susan and Bill were hosting this spiritual healing workshop. On the last day of class, Susan talked to the instructor about her husband, Bill. She asked if we could do a healing on him. He was going to have a triple bypass operation on his heart. Bill and Susan were very concerned (as they should be) about the outcome of the operation. We all agreed that we would work on Bill. Similar to before, other students were selected for positions alongside the body and I was told to work on the most challenging healing area; which was in this case, Bill's heart. We were six healers proceeding as a group to perform spiritual healing on the whole person.

Working on his heart with my eyes closed, I could see his heart pumping blood. I visualized all his arteries and vessels being cleansed of anything that could obstruct his blood flow to the heart. Eventually, I felt Bill's heart beat changing to a heavier beat.

Just then Bill started to cry out, "Oh, my heart!"

His loud cry brought me out of meditation and visualization. I took my hands off of him and stepped back. He grabbed his chest and once again cried, "Oh, my heart!"

Everyone stopped and moved back as Susan rushed to his side. She asked him what she could do.

"My heart is burning. Everything in my chest is burning."

Bill was helped downstairs and out into the yard where their car was parked. She opened the hatch door and had Bill brought down to lie on a thin mattress that was in the rear of the car.

Lying down in the car, Bill said he felt a little better. I asked Susan why not call 911? She said it was faster for her to bring him to the hospital, as an ambulance would have to come up the mountain through the narrow winding dirt roads to find their place. Susan drove speeding down the hill toward the hospital. I watched the car as it kicked up dust from the dirt road and thought, *Maybe healing from six healers was too much for him*. And then I thought, *I was the one who worked on his heart and chest*.

I directed all healing for his wellbeing, wherever it was needed. I visualized Bill and said a little prayer that he would come out of this all right.

We all went back inside to learn more of what the instructor's company had to offer. We learned about other seminars and where they would be located.

After this session was over, the instructor said, "If anyone has to leave it's all right to go. Those of you who want to wait until we hear about how Bill is doing are welcome to stay."

I decided to stay and see if Bill was going to be okay. The instructor said, "Let's have a moment of silence for Bill."

Everyone, in their own way, wished him healing and a safe return.

Just as we finished two cars drove up the driveway. A large man stepped out from his car wearing a chef's hat and carrying a lot of packages as he headed for the door of the house. Susan got out of her car carrying two packages and Bill carried a bushel basket filled with something. The three of them, Bill, Susan and the Chef, carried their packages and the bushel basket of something into the kitchen with big smiles on their faces.

Bill turned to us and said, "I have something to say to everyone. "Thank you, I thank you, I thank you."

Susan said, "Do you know how hard it is to find a fresh bushel of shrimp," and then she laughed.

Susan told us when Bill arrived at the hospital he was asleep and they took him from the car on a stretcher. As they brought him into the hospital he opened his eyes and smiled at her. Inside the doctor was waiting for him and they immediately took Bill into an examining room.

After some tests, the doctor told Susan, "You know the triple bypass that Bill needed? We are going to forget it. Something amazing has happened. Somehow all blockages flushed out of him! If you believe in miracles then this is one! I don't think this has ever been reported medically before. He wanted to keep Bill for a few days just to keep an eye on him, but he insisted on returning home."

Susan said, "I told the doctor the healers at our house must have helped to make this happen; particularly one healer, Frank, who worked on Bill's heart."

Bill spoke then, saying, "I was going to tell you privately, Frank, but now you know."

Bill grabbed me and hugged me, lifting me off my feet saying, "I thank you, very much. My family thanks you very much. I bought a basket full of shrimp and hired a cook to come home with me. Frank, I want you to eat as much shrimp as you want, and whatever else you want."

The group started to clap for me and I thanked Bill and Susan for the compliment.

"I believe everything that has happened was a joint effort of all the healers in the room. I'm just so glad that I could participate in these healings."

The instructor said, "Yes, I believe all of you have played a part in these healings that have taken place."

Everyone clapped and many patted me on my back. After they stopped clapping, I said, "I have something to say." You could have heard a pin drop, it became so quiet.

"As to the shrimp you brought, I appreciate the gesture of eating all I want, but I will give my share of the shrimp to everyone else. It is the only thing I am allergic to!"

Everyone laughed. Bill said we have plenty of chicken and turkey.

"Let's celebrate," Susan said.

The cook started preparing the meal and the table was set. We all sat and talked about happy things, and before long, our meal was ready to eat. We all ate and ate. It was a delicious meal prepared by fine people. The lady from New York asked me, once more, if I would like to go into business with her.

"It would cost you nothing," she said.

I smiled and thanked her. "New York is a little too far away from where I live now. I'm sorry."

She gave me a big hug and said, "God bless you."

When it was time to leave, the instructor asked to talk with me. I followed him into another room. He asked if I would reconsider and go to work for him. I thanked him for asking me again.

"No, but if I were going to work for anyone it would be your company. Right now my mission is simple. I will try to help everyone who comes to me."

As I walked toward the door to leave, all the people in the seminar were in one line waiting to hug me and shake my hand. With tears in my eyes, I said thank you and goodbye to everyone.

As I started out of the driveway, Susan ran out of the house toward my car.

"My daughter fell off a swing on her face at a neighbor's house and is unconscious."

"She is all right," I assured her.

She jumped in her car and sped away down the hill. I started the drive home while sending healing to Susan's daughter. I knew she hit her face but I pictured a girl who was happy. What a lucky little girl! Everything was going to be all right.

About an hour down the road I drove into a rest area and called Susan. She said she just came from the hospital. She told me how lucky her daughter was and that she only had minor bruises. She was even laughing about what happened.

"She will have no scars, thank God," Susan said.

I told Susan I would come back if I were needed.

"Thank you, but everything is fine now. I have a husband and daughter, both healthy and well. You must have been praying for my daughter."

"Yes, and I'm sure everyone else did, too."

I was about one hour away from her, but I would have driven back if I were needed. I arrived home safely and after a good night sleep, I started another pleasant day in my life.

Twenty-Three

My friend Andi and I have had a long lasting relationship ever since she hired me to paint her house in Plymouth, MA, when I was a commercial and residential painting contractor. For many years now, we have lived together in my house in Taunton, MA. She is a beautiful person, inside and out.

Over the years, Andi's mother, Georgia, was a great part of our life. When we went shopping, to restaurants, or just for a ride, we would pick up Georgia and take her with us. She lived 25 miles away in an appartment complex for the elderly. It was a nice place and she enjoyed living there.

Through the years I grew very close to Georgia and cared about her. As the years passed, Andi noticed that her mother was not managing very well and was forgetting to eat. After consulting with a visiting nurse and Georgia's physician about her mother's condition Andi, along with her sister and brother, decided that Georgia should now go to a nursing home. Andi and her sister Chris, who drove up from Connecticut, visited several nursing homes. They selected one approximately 40 minutes from my house in Taunton.

Andi visited her mother frequently and I would visit with her weekly. We would pick Georgia up and go for rides, do some shopping, and then go to Andi's house in Plymouth. Although they lived out of state, Andi kept her sister and brother apprised of their mother's condition on a regular basis. This Greek family was very close. Andi's father died one month after she was born, so her mother assumed the roles of both mother and father to her children. Georgia helped her children attend college on the modest wages she earned. She was the type of mother who would always put her children first. If she had a few extra dollars at the end of the month, she would send it along to her children in college. Georgia was a unique person and I liked everything about her. She was a survivor.

One evening while Andi and I were home having dinner, she received a telephone call from the nurse practitioner at her mother's nursing home. Andi was told her mother was in pain but they did not know why. Her oxygen level was also low. I heard Andi tell the nurse to tell her mother she was on her way there.

Upon hanging up the telephone, Andi immediately said, "My mother is not well and I need to see her now." We prepared to leave. It was snowing outside. Although I drove quickly, it seemed to Andi like an eternity

When we arrived at the nursing home, we walked directly to her mother's room. A nurse was sitting by

Georgia's bed and holding her hand. She said to us, "I'm so glad you're here."

Andi asked if her mother was going to be all right. The nurse shook her head no.

Georgia's eyes were closed. Her breathing was heavy, and at times, it seemed she wasn't breathing at all. Andi held one of her hands while I held the other. I spoke to her silently with both my mind and my heart, *As you go to a better place, I will remember you.* I looked at Andi who had tears streaming down her face. She knew the end was near.

I felt Georgia squeeze my hand. I had a feeling she knew it was all right for her to leave. I looked at her lying in bed, hardly breathing.

All I could say to her was "It will be all right."

Andi and I stayed at her mother's bedside. As the minutes went by, Georgia's breathing got worse with long pauses between breaths, but she continued to squeeze my hand. I closed my eyes and could see her pulling my hand and taking me with her to a place next to a large hill. It was dark, but with enough light so that I could see the bushes, trees and large rocks. Just in front of us was an entrance to a tunnel. The entrance glowed with a beautiful white light.

The rays of light enveloped us and I felt like I was being transformed back into a young man. I felt great and alive. Still holding my hand, Georgia pulled me forward and we both walked into the lit tunnel. I looked at her as she held my hand. She was alive and well.

We had walked into the tunnel entrance a good distance when I hit something. It was an invisible wall that stopped me from going in any further. However, Georgia walked easily through this barrier. She pulled on my hand as she looked at me, but I could go no further. I let go of her hand and said, "Don't be afraid, your husband, your daughter Chris, other family members and friends are ahead of you."

I watched Georgia as she walked slowly through the brightly lit tunnel. She stopped and turned around to look at me, then looked ahead as the beams of light surrounded her. She gave me a smile and a little wave and walked further into the light until I could no longer see her.

When I opened my eyes we were back in the nursing home again. I was holding her hand as she took her last breath. I thanked her for taking me to that tunnel with the bright white lights. Now when my time comes, I will not be afraid and will go willingly into the beautiful white light alone.

Twenty-Four

One day when I stopped at a red light, I noticed some men and women coming out of a nursing home. I had a feeling I was needed. I parked my truck on the side of the road that faced the nursing home so I could watch the people as they sat outdoors.

The staff appeared to be doing a good job caring for the patients, although everyone looked like they had lost the bright spark of life and hope. As I observed each person, I prayed for the power of understanding that this is not the end, but the beginning of a new adventure.

I kept sending out the thought, *Peace within, happiness and good memories.* I wanted these words to penetrate into each person. As I continued to observe them, I noticed they started smiling and acting happy.

As I was saying a prayer for understanding and happiness, I noticed a tall, thin, elderly lady being escorted to her seat. There was no expression on her face as she sat up in her chair, looking straight ahead. Her eyes didn't blink. She seemed lost in her memories.

The Silent Healer

I saw a tall man sit down next to her. He could have been her husband, brother or friend. I watched him as he talked to her. I couldn't hear the words that were spoken to her, but his lips were moving as his hands were stroking her hair and touching her face. I could feel the love coming from him. He hugged her and whispered something in her ear. He looked at her for a long time, and then lowered his head. I could see him wiping away tears.

As I watched, my eyes were blinded with tears as well. The woman just sat there, looking straight ahead, with no expression on her face. It seemed as though she was not receiving the feeling of love directed at her. I prayed to God, Jesus, the angels, and anyone else who could help. I wanted to undo what was wrong and help her come back and be present to the love and the life around her.

I continued to watch as the staff started to move everyone inside. I watched this one lady with great interest as she was escorted back into the building. Her visitor wiped his glasses and walked away. I then drove away.

The elderly lady and man certainly captured my heart. I worked the rest of the day with tears still coming down my face. That night I meditated, and sent healing to those in need. I visualized myself being with the elderly lady at the nursing home. She was sitting, looking straight ahead, as she did before. I stood behind her and placed my hands on her shoulders. When I felt the healing vibrations and a surge of energy flowing inside me, I then placed my hands on her head. I asked God for many good things to happen. I moved my hands down to her ears and paused. I then placed one hand on her forehead and the other hand on her neck. I continued to pray for a long time and then fell asleep.

The next day, I drove to the nursing home, parked across the street, and watched as the people were being helped to their seats. I again wished everyone peace within, happiness and good memories.

Then I saw the elderly lady come out of the building with her male visitor. He helped her into a chair, pulled another chair close to her and sat down. He brushed her hair with the back of his hand, touched her face and spoke to her. She sat motionless, just looking straight ahead. I watched him as he kept talking to her and put his head on her left shoulder near her face. This certainly touched my heart. My tears started flowing as they did the day before.

I watched him speaking to her with his hands touching her face, shoulders, and then holding her hands. As I sat in my truck watching, I was not aware of anything else around me, only what was unfolding in front of me. I closed my eyes and went into deep meditation. I whispered, *if it's not against anything holy, allow this lady to come back to this time and place; to be able to hear and talk, understand and have feelings, show emotions and smile. Let her come back so that love can be shared.*

I opened my eyes and realized I must have been meditating for long time. This lady and the others were being helped back inside.

I drove away thinking, *where did the time go*? I returned to work to continue painting a large house. I worked until just before dark. As I was putting the paint and brushes away in my truck, I looked at the house and was surprised to see how much I had painted that day.

When I got home and relaxed, I told Andi what had gone on the last two days. She listened intently as I described what had happened and how I felt. When I finished, Andi responded,

"All you can do is pray for her, and also for the gentleman who comes to visit her each day."

That night, before sleeping, as always, I meditated and sent healing to many people including the elderly lady and her male visitor.

In the morning when I drove back to work, I passed the nursing home and questioned myself as to why I was so connected to this lady, and to her visitor, whom I sensed was a unique person. I had performed hundreds of healings, yet I felt so drawn to this one lady and knew I must help her. Although it had only been two days that I had tried to help, it seemed like a much longer time had elapsed. I had tried my best as I had given my heart and shed many tears.

On the third day, I watched, prayed and wondered how many more days I would come, and whether a miracle would happen. The people were escorted to their chairs and made comfortable. Bless the people who take care of other people; they are so greatly needed.

I saw the elderly lady being helped out of the doorway by the same gentleman. Again, she sat in the same chair with her visitor sitting beside her. I watched as he spoke to her. I will never know what he said as I could only see his lips moving. The expression on his face showed love and hope

I closed my eyes and the first thing I thought was, *Please help this lady.*

When I opened my eyes and looked, she turned and looked at me. Then she looked at her male visitor and spoke to him.

He stood up and I heard his words, even from across the street.

"Oh my God!"

She stood up. He hugged her. She hugged him. I saw a man run into the nursing home and come out with a lot of people who were hugging, kissing and crying. Everyone was so happy!

If I had died at that moment, I would have left this world with the greatest feeling of happiness one could ever achieve. I could see how happy and alive the lady looked as the man with her was crying tears of joy.

I started my truck and drove away, wiping the tears from my eyes. I headed for work and thought, *It took three days for this miracle to happen. I'm so lucky that I was allowed to play a part in this lady's life.*

The Silent Healer

I was drawn to her with such a strong connection to help. Now the desire to help her had been released. I was so happy that this miracle allowed this woman and this man more quality time together.

Twenty-Five

I always enjoyed going to church. When I was younger, I sometimes went to as many as three different services on the same Sunday.

On this particular day, I walked into the church and down the center aisle to the fourth seat from the front. This is where I like to sit every Sunday, with my lady friend, Andi, beside me. Once I was comfortable I opened my hymnal to an inside page. There was a sticker inside which read, "In memory of Matilda St. Martin by Frank St. Martin." Andi's hymnal read, "In memory of Lillian Kable by Frank St. Martin." What a coincidence, I thought to myself. Was this just by chance? I had just been dreaming about my grandmother and my Aunt Lil.

Many things I have thought of and dreamt about have happened. Writing this book is one of my dreams so I can reach others wherever they may be. I have a feeling the best years are still to come. In the years ahead, I believe I will help more people than I have helped in the past. I look forward to meeting all the people I have not met yet.

One Sunday evening I went to bed a little early. I visualized and meditated on past events that I had with my grandmother and my aunt. Two hours later I opened my eyes. I was very pleased at what had transpired in those two hours. I had seen a movie of myself being born and all the smiling people I came to know and help heal. I also visualized people whom I had not yet met but I felt I had given them healing as well.

From the beginning of my life, until this very moment, I feel like I have experienced it all. I am very pleased with my life's events. I am so pleased that I know and feel what I have done is what I was supposed to do and will continue to do. I call myself a silent healer because the healing I've done has always had to be done silently, as my grandmother had cautioned me to do.

In the early days of my life, I was told to say only God or Jesus does miracle healing. If anyone else, especially a young boy, was involved in a miracle healing, people would have burned our house down because of the fear of black magic. We have come a long way since then, yet doctors and healers are still not working together. Hopefully, they will someday.

There is energy and light that I feel and see when I touch a person who is in front of me for healing. This also occurs when I visualize a person in front of me who may live many miles away. The light that surrounds me, and whomever I'm told to work on, is not always a white light. Most people believe that it's only the white light that can heal. Of all my years being involved in healing, since the age of eight until now, I have always experienced the white light as well as a golden colored light. I've tried to understand why some are in a white light and some in a golden light. I am no closer to the answer than I was when I started. I accept, without question, the light that surrounds me, and the person who is receiving the healing.

Each healing situation may take a different approach. I have been doing distant healing for a very long time. The results have been very effective. It does not matter how far a person actually is in distance away from me. I live south of Boston but I have done distant healings on people as far away as California and Europe. Every person that I visualize and meditate on is standing or sitting next to me. I see this in my mind every time I need to focus on an individual.

With distant healing, I helped a lady to survive on the day she planned to commit suicide. Early one morning, Barbara, a friend of mine for over fifteen years at that time, came to my house and was frantically knocking on my door. Barbara was visibly upset and started telling me about her friend, Jan. She was talking very rapidly, tears streaming down her face. I told Barbara to sit down and gave her a glass of water, which helped her to relax. I asked Barbara to speak slowly so I could understand what she was trying to tell me and be able to help.

With more tears in her eyes, she began, "Frank, I need your help now! Jan, a friend of mine, has been very depressed. In the past three weeks, I have noticed a change in her behavior. She and I have been friends for over thirty years. We have shared a great deal during that time. Every week we go out to new restaurants and stores and stop by each other's house to visit."

As Barbara was sharing this with me, I observed a smile on her face. Then her mood changed.

"I should have come to you sooner to ask for your help. I didn't and I should have known better. " Barbara continued. " I feel so guilty now."

Sobbing uncontrollably, Barbara pleaded, "I don't want to lose Jan."

Before I could ask her why Jan wanted to end her life, Barbara sobbed more loudly. I comforted her as I listened and felt her sorrow. I had tears in my eyes as well. I felt sorry for Barbara, as this was the first time I had ever seen her cry. As she sobbed, and was unable to talk, I thought of the wonderful things Barbara had done for other people over the years.

I offered her a cup of tea to help calm her. I was then able to ask her how I could be of help.

"Please speak slowly."

After taking a deep breath, Barbara said, "I don't know what to do to help her. My good friend says she is going to commit suicide and she won't let me in her house. She won't even come to the door. I talked to her on the telephone a few days ago. She thanked me for being her friend all these years and then she said, 'The time has come. I just want to end it all, and I will.' Jan called me this morning and told me not to go to her house and knock on her door anymore because she would not answer. Jan's family and other friends are being treated the same way."

Barbara was convinced Jan would commit suicide. "It could be as soon as today or tomorrow." As Barbara spoke, she looked at me then looked down at the floor, with tears streaming down her face.

I asked Barbara if she had a picture of Jan. I also asked her how old Jan was, the color of her eyes and hair, how much she weighed, and what time she usually goes to bed? Barbara had all the information that was necessary to do a distant healing. I told her I would do my best to help save Jan and that I needed a few days to try to contact Jan using my mind to communicate with her. If I can make this contact Jan will get better.

In the meantime, I urged Barbara to try to talk to Jan. "Even if she ignores you, continue to try to communicate with her. This will afford me more time to make a min- connection with Jan." Barbara agreed. As she was leaving, she said she would pay me whatever amount of money I asked. Of course, I would never charge a fee from this good friend of mine.

Although I had a busy schedule that day, I changed it in order to focus exclusively on this life and death situation with Jan.

I reviewed all the information Barbara had shared with me. I looked at Jan's photograph and saw she was an attractive lady with a wonderful smile. I wondered what had occurred in her life that would cause her to feel so depressed and so unhappy. I strongly believe we are what we think. When I interact with clients I point this out to them so they can understand that if they are to change their lives, they need to change their thoughts.

I went to my office and sat down in my reclining chair. I looked at Jan's photograph then closed my eyes. I visualized Jan and tried to connect with her mind.

I continued by asking Jan in my mind, *Tell me if you can hear me?*

I concentrated deeply into Jan's third eye, which centered in the middle of her forehead. My words and feelings were directed into her mind. I wish Jan had already been a client of mine, as it would have made it easier for me to connect with her thinking. Throughout the day I attempted to communicate with Jan, but received no response that I could act upon. Barbara called me and told me where Jan lived. I shared with Barbara that I had not yet achieved any communication from her.

After speaking with Barbara, I drove to Jan's house and parked on the side of the road. In my mind I was speaking to Jan. I told her *Do not hurt yourself.* I repeated this statement over and over again. Then I asked Jan to open her mind and listen to me. I was going to knock on her door, but then I remembered what Barbara had previously said, that Jan would not open the door even for her family or close friends. I decided to go back home and work on her from there.

I went back into the office and sat down in my recliner to meditate and visualize Jan being calm and comfortable so that she could be receptive to my suggestions. I wanted her to reply to my questions through our mind-connection. I continued to try to connect with Jan throughout the night. I spent the next morning meditating and visualizing what I wanted to happen regarding Jan. I had a feeling that time was running out for me and for Jan. I asked God and Jesus to help me and to use me as a healer as had been done so many times before.

"Please, I thank you, God. I thank you. I thank you, Jesus, I thank you."

I called upon all the people in my life who had passed away. Mostly everyone knew me as The Silent Healer. I really felt in my heart it could not hurt to ask. Then I called Barbara and asked if she had talked to Jan. She told me she had called all day and night; probably fifty times, but Jan did not respond. Barbara also drove to Jan's house and stood at her door and talked to her for hours, but Jan never answered her. Then Barbara went to each window and talked to Jan again, but she didn't respond. Barbara told me she was not going to give up on Jan. She was going to buy two coffees and two muffins, sit on the step, and talk to Jan.

The Silent Healer

Barbara yelled and sobbed on the phone. "I refuse to give up on her! Please help my friend, Jan!"

I told her I was working very hard to save her friend. With tears and a thank you, Barbara hung up. I returned to my meditation and visualization until I finally made contact with Jan.

"Who are you?" Jan asked.

"I am a friend. Tell me why you want to harm yourself?"

"I just want to end it all. Even with my family and friends, I feel so alone. I know I can end this life of mine, and I can do it today."

"No you cannot!" I shouted back at her. "Everyone you know loves you and wants you to live!"

I then asked Jan, "Do you believe in God and Jesus?"

"Yes."

Then you must know that Scripture teaches, "*Thou shalt not kill.*"

I told Jan that her close friend, Barbara, had stopped working the last two days and will probably lose her job.

Jan replied, "Barbara has come here day and night, talking to me while walking around my house and looking into each window. I never answered her. I would have ended my life, but Barbara was here day and night talking and talking and talking to me, and crying and crying."

I told Jan that she had accepted me into her mind, and I have accepted her into my mind.

"I have never met you, but I want you to live. Do not harm yourself!"

Then I heard Jan say, "Oh my God! It is as if a veil has been lifted up from my face to the top of my head."

I shouted, "Hallelujah! I have heard this statement many times before! Jan, you are now healed! You no longer want to harm yourself. Am I right?"

"Yes! Yes!" was her reply.

I told Jan I was going to call Barbara to go to her house and take her out to eat or just for a ride.

"Okay?"

Jan excitedly responded, "Yes!"

I called Barbara and shared what had happened. She cried and asked, "Should I go to Jan's house now?"

"Yes, Jan is waiting for you."

A few days later Barbara came to my house.

"I thank you and all of Jan's family and friends thank you. How much do we owe you?"

I looked at Barbara's bright eyes and happy face.

"Nobody owes me anything," I said. "I was happy to help you and your friend, Jan."

Twenty-Six

The first time I saw a blue rose I was in deep meditation. With my eyes closed, I visualized that I was standing in a beautiful valley filled with an array of colored flowers. Some of the colors I had never seen before. Even the small bushes scattered throughout the valley were brightly colored. The beauty and blending of the colors throughout this place were indescribable. It was a world of its own. This enchanting place will only show its beauty to those who are worthy of seeking it out. The farther I looked into the valley, the more of God's beauty I could see. Beyond the trees was a large lake, and as the sun touched the water, bright flashes of light reflected back like hundreds of stars on a clear night.

As I was contemplating this breathtaking and brightly colored vision, I became aware that if I opened my eyes it would all be gone. I chose to keep my eyes closed since I felt so comfortable and safe. I continued with my meditation and visualization when unexpectedly I had an apparition of a blue rose.

"Many have come before you and many will come after you," I heard whispered in my ear. I turned to see who was whispering, but no one was there. Upon reflection, I came to realize that the meaning of this message was for me to share this beautiful pristine holy place with others. I knew in my mind and heart that the blue rose had a significant meaning. I knew that through meditation and visualization it would be possible to enter into this world of love, kindness and forgiveness, and once here, I would find the blue rose.

I looked up at a rock platform that led to a cave; I knew this was where I must go. I climbed straight up. I thought I could rest at each path on my way up to the entrance of the cave but the more I climbed the more I felt the need to continue on. The feeling I had within me was warm and loving.

As I climbed faster up the mountain, I suddenly realized that although I had been pulling myself upward by grabbing onto small bushes and trees, my heart rate was calm and I was not tired. I pressed my feet against a small tree to resume my balance on the steep incline.

Suddenly, I was aware of a golden light surrounding me. This light extended about two feet beyond every part of my body. It was a good feeling. I felt I was protected and loved all at the same time. I also have been aware of this golden light around me while in the process of healing others and saving lives.

I walked forward into the light and the entrance of the cave. I sensed I was going to experience something wonderful once I entered. I expected to see a single, or perhaps several, blue roses growing there. When I looked into the cave, it was not what I expected.

The beautiful blue rose was not in the ground. It was suspended in the air about five feet above a stone floor! All the colors of the rainbow were vibrating within the cave walls. Not a sound could be heard. The feeling of oneness and of infinite power and love overwhelmed me. I was experiencing something magical, even if only for a short time. I looked at the blue rose and knew it understood what I felt.

In that moment, I thought my eyes were playing tricks on me. The original blue rose divided itself. I was now looking at two identical blue roses. One blue rose came forward and stopped in front of me. I looked back at the blue rose further in the cave. I now understood the beautiful vibrating colors within the cave walls were the protectors of the blue roses. I felt I was in a holy place. Then I heard a voice.

"Take the blue rose. Give it to those who ask for help. This blue rose will multiply and you will not be without one. With the gifts that you possess, use this blue rose to help others. I hold you to this promise."

I reached out and gently took the blue rose that stood in the air before me. A deep feeling of love and belonging enveloped me. With tears of happiness, I looked up and asked the blue rose, "Can I ever come back to see you again?"

"Yes."

I knew I had to leave now. I followed the golden light on the ground. I held this magical blue rose close to my heart while walking away. As I descended, I paused and looked back. The rainbow of colors first vibrated around the blue rose, and then continued high into the universe. The beauty was spectacular!

I opened my eyes. I looked at the clock. I had been meditating for five hours. It was so real! My eyes were still wet with tears. I then realized that I was still holding the blue rose on my chest next to my heart. I sat in my chair quietly, very still, hardly breathing.

I heard a voice clearly say to me, "I hold you to this promise."

My God, this has really happened!

As I looked at the blue rose I was holding, it just melted into my hand and disappeared.

****

Whenever I return to the holy place where I found the blue rose, I am reminded that it was given to me to become a part of my life and to always pray for others.

Frank St. Martin

The Message of the Blue Rose

Remember, give love to yourself first,
and then you will know how to give love to others.
Remember, be kind to yourself first,
and then you will know how to be kind to others.
Remember, forgive yourself first,
and then you will know how to forgive others.
I hold you to this promise, forever.

I Believe
By Frank St. Martin

I have a good friend;
I never saw him.
I never heard his voice, but I felt him within.
I know he is around me,
My heart tells me so.
Many times I've been touched by him,
Yet only I know.
When I take a trip, he comes with me.
When I feel alone, I think I am,
But I am not.

ABOUT FRANK ST. MARTIN

Frank St. Martin has been a healer since childhood. His grandmother feared for his safety if his "gifts" were talked about so he became "The Silent Healer."

As a young man, Frank joined the Navy and became a ship's head cook and traveled the world. After his discharge he worked for several blue-collar companies before starting his own successful commercial and residential painting business, as well as several other companies.

Frank always helped those in need, and would hire people who had difficulty keeping a job. He would provide them with clean clothing and expected them to put in an honest day's work. He was successful in helping turn around the lives of many people he recruited.

He is a multi-tasker, who at the age of 80, is still working and healing others. Frank devotes a great deal of time to any project he selects. He manages to overcome challenges by working more aggressively, and is always reading and studying to improve himself. He believes in putting in more than 110%, determined to be the best in a given situation. His healing "gifts" have helped hundreds of people over the years.

Frank enjoys gardening and is an expert woodworker. He lives with his companion, Andi, in Taunton, MA

Credits:
Commissioned Healer of the American Federation of Spiritualist Churches
Certified Consulting Hypnotist
5 - PATH® Hypnotherapist
7th Path Self-Hypnosis® Teacher
Reiki Master

Mr. St. Martin is a certified member of the National Guild of Hypnotists (NGH).

Feel free to contact him with questions regarding Hypnotism, Hypnotherapy, Distant Healing and Reiki.

(774) 773-9153 or (508) 822-9000
www.stmartinhypnotherapyandreikicenter.com

Acknowledgments

I express my deepest gratitude to the following people:

Mary Carriere for graciously agreeing to type my handwritten notes into manuscript form which resulted in a 500-plus page first draft of the manuscript. Without her assistance this book would not have evolved.

Ginny Weissman, my editor, who spent countless hours reviewing and editing the content of the manuscript resulting in the final draft of the book.

Andrianne Maniatis, my friend and companion, for her constant support, as well as reading and correcting the proof along with another friend (you know who you are) who wishes to remain anonymous.

Paul Burt, at Pen & Publish, Inc., for guiding us through the publishing process.

All the family members, friends and clients whose lives have touched mine and are an important part of this memoir.

www.ingramcontent.com/pod-product-compliance
Lightning Source LLC
Chambersburg PA
CBHW031249290426
44109CB00012B/496